YOU ARE GODS

YOU ARE GODS

ON NATURE AND SUPERNATURE

DAVID BENTLEY HART

University of Notre Dame Press
Notre Dame, Indiana

Published by the University of Notre Dame Press
Notre Dame, Indiana 46556
undpress.nd.edu

Published in the United States of America

Library of Congress Control Number: 2021948751

ISBN: 978-0-268-20193-7 (Hardback)
ISBN: 978-0-268-20194-4 (Paperback)
ISBN: 978-0-268-20192-0 (WebPDF)
ISBN: 978-0-268-20195-1 (Epub)

For Alfred Turnipseed

अयम् आत्मा ब्रह्म

ἀπεκρίθη αὐτοῖς ὁ Ἰησοῦς· οὐκ ἔστιν γεγραμμένον ἐν τῷ νόμῳ ὑμῶν ὅτι
ἐγὼ εἶπα· θεοί ἐστε; εἰ ἐκείνους εἶπεν θεοὺς πρὸς οὓς ὁ λόγος τοῦ θεοῦ
ἐγένετο, καὶ οὐ δύναται λυθῆναι ἡ γραφή, ὃν ὁ πατὴρ ἡγίασεν καὶ
ἀπέστειλεν εἰς τὸν κόσμον ὑμεῖς λέγετε ὅτι βλασφημεῖς, ὅτι εἶπον·
υἱὸς τοῦ θεοῦ εἰμι;

———

[Jesus answered them, "Is it not written in your Law 'I said, "You are
gods?"' If he called those to whom God's Logos came 'gods,' and if scripture
cannot be dissolved, do you then tell him whom the Father sanctified and
sent out into the cosmos, 'You blaspheme!' just because I have said
'I am the Son of God?'"]

—John 10:34–36

. . . ἀπεκρίθη αὐτοῖς καὶ εἶπεν οὐκ ἔρχεται ἡ βασιλεία τοῦ θεοῦ μετὰ
παρατηρήσεως, ἰδοὺ ὧδε ἤ ἐκεῖ, ἰδοὺ γὰρ ἡ βασιλεία τοῦ θεοῦ
ἐντὸς ὑμῶν ἐστιν.

———

[. . . he answered them and said, "The Kingdom does not come as
something one observes, nor will persons say, 'Look: Here it is' or
'There it is'; for look: The Kingdom of God is inside of you."]

—Luke 17:20–21

CONTENTS

Introduction   xi

ONE
Waking the Gods: *Theosis* as Reason's Natural End   1

TWO
The Treasure of Delight: Nicholas of Cusa on Infinite Desire   21

THREE
That Judgment Whereby You Judge: Beauty and Discernment   35

FOUR
Pia Fraus: Our Words and God's Truth   51

FIVE
Geist's Kaleidoscope: Some Questions for Cyril O'Regan   63

SIX
The Chiasmus: The Created Supernatural
and the Natural Divine   97

Notes   125
Index   137

INTRODUCTION

In recent years, the theological—and, more specifically, Roman Catholic—question of "the supernatural" has made an astonishing return from seeming oblivion. Until very recently indeed, most theologians with any knowledge of the question's history had been working under the impression that the issue was more or less settled, and that the early modern theology of supernature and nature that had been briefly dominant in Catholic thought—the infamous "two-tier" system of "manualist" or "commentary" or "second scholastic" Thomism—had been decisively defeated by the far superior and more orthodox theologies of grace that had displaced it. Certainly, those two or three remarkable generations of systematic theologians who made the twentieth century one of the genuinely golden epochs of Roman Catholic thought seemed to have been able to accomplish as much as they did precisely because they had freed themselves from the desiccating atmosphere of that tradition. After all, as we had all been led to believe, the theological proposals of the manualist schools had been curious anomalies in the history of Christian thought, so alien to the whole of patristic tradition, and to most of the mediaeval, and so plainly irreconcilable with cardinal tenets of classical Christian thought and dogma, that they were incapable of producing theology of any particular range or substance, or of exercising much influence outside the small circle in which they had been gestated. Taken together, they appeared to constitute a depressingly sterile system, one that was eerily immune to any kind of enrichment or healthy development, inasmuch as any attempt at either could only expose its internal incoherence; at most, the system could be curated, defended, and endlessly reiterated by the small but indefatigable faction devoted to it.

It seemed only natural, therefore, to suppose that, once something better, fuller, finer, and more rational had come along (call it *la nouvelle théologie* or *ressourcement* or the patristic restoration or even "the Eastward turn"), nothing as morbidly barren, impoverished, and unattractive as the manualist tradition would ever again have the power or allure to inspire any sane soul's allegiance. Why, after all, would anyone want to set aside the lush, velvety, heady wines of Catholicism's magnificent twentieth-century theological renaissance to quaff the thin, acrid waters of Wormwood from a rusting tin cup? Why, in particular, would today's students of Thomas want to retreat from the repristinated figure of modern research—an inheritor of the fathers and a truly *mediaeval* metaphysician possessed of genuine synthetic genius—to recover the caricature produced by manualism, which spoke in an attenuated early modern language of causality, presumed an early modern vision of desacralized nature, and practiced an early modern style of propositional logic? Surely the whole sordid episode of commentary Thomism could now be written off as a closed chapter in theological history, a curious anecdote that had briefly interrupted the authentic narrative of Catholic dogma and theology. Alas, it was not so. *Die Wiederkehr des Verdrängten* is a law as much of institutional as of personal psychology. And so now this once seemingly very dead tradition is enjoying a revival (or, better, recrudescence) in certain traditionalist Catholic sects, most especially here in America, where some odd perversity of our national temperament forbids us from ever allowing any ideological project or alliance, no matter how diseased, to die with dignity.

Why this has happened I cannot really guess. It turns out that all those prejudices that those who came after the perceived fall of the two-tierist systems were taught to hold, when examined closely and scrupulously, are not mere prejudices at all, but simple statements of fact. So the system's return is an altogether shocking reversal of all expectations, rather as if some adventurer long thought dead and buried (or eaten, or frozen, or drowned) in some unknown and far-flung quarter of the uncharted wilds—one who has been pronounced legally deceased, whose estate has already been apportioned to his heirs, and whose wife of many years is now wed to another man—were suddenly to appear at the door of his old home, gray and gaunt and marked by the ravages of time and misfortune, but very much alive and adamantly demanding the restoration of everything he has lost in his absence. In either case, that of the obsolete theological system or that of the truant adventurer, the return has come too late in the day to be a cause of much rejoicing; the newer generations of theologians, the heirs of the estate, the widow *secundum legem*, even some older theologians formed in the abandoned system, or even some of the forgotten explorer's lifelong friends—all of them are more likely to find the new situation far more of a predicament than a blessing. I tend to think that the current enthusiasm for early modern Thomism is a matter for psychological or sociological investigation rather than something that can be explained in terms of logic or of some genuine spiritual imperative. But I cannot say that this is so with perfect confidence, since I cannot enter imaginatively into minds that find, say, Garrigou-Lagrange's books deeply moving, or even vaguely palatable. The whole phenomenon must remain a mystery to me, one whose more occult causes will forever be veiled from my eyes behind a curtain of Baroque fustian (or perhaps sickly puce).

If, by the way, my language to this point seems a bit weighted toward one side of the debate, I can only assure readers that my motives are entirely sincere and disinterested. I am not Roman Catholic, after all, and so none of this concerns me personally; and, really, the future of Catholic theology is of no consequence to me at all. The topic interests me only insofar as it raises issues of a more general kind regarding the contents of Christian faith. Precisely because I regard the "two-tier" understanding of nature and supernature as irreparably defective, and in fact among the most defective understandings of Christianity imaginable—in many ways the diametric opposite of everything the Christian story has to say about reality and about the relation of creation to God and about the person of Christ—the unwelcome return of this superannuated vagabond provokes me just enough to make me want to advance an altogether different picture. Perhaps I cannot lay the ghost of two-tierism, or exorcise it from modern theological discourse. But I can, at the very least, take advantage of the moment.

The essays collected here were all written within a relatively short span, each for a particular occasion, but all in pursuit of much the same intellectual quarry. Each in its way addresses the topic of the "natural supernatural," and all were shaped by the same stream of reflections. The first, "Waking the Gods," was originally delivered in somewhat different form at Fordham University for the Patterson Triennial Conference, "Faith, Reason, and Theosis," in June 2019; the original version of the lecture is printed in *Faith, Reason, and Theosis*, ed. Aristotle Papanikolaou and George Demacopoulos (New York: Fordham University Press, 2022). Its relevance for this volume is obvious, as it lays out both the issue of the supernatural and the incorrigible logical flaws in the two-tier position. The second, "The Treasure of Delight," was delivered at the University of Notre Dame at the conference "Cusanus Today" in September 2019. It rather seamlessly resumes one of the principal themes of the preceding essay: to wit, the impossibility of any spiritual nature resting content in a merely natural end. The third, "That Judgment Whereby You Judge," was delivered at Holy Cross Seminary and Hellenic College as the annual Florovsky Lecture of the Orthodox Theological Society of America in October 2018. Its relevance here is that it is an exercise in erasing any hard and fast partition between the worldly experience of transcendental values and the eschatological experience of divine judgment. The fourth, "*Pia Fraus*," was an address for a private society devoted to philosophical ethics delivered in December 2018, though I have revised it here; the original version was published in the Spring 2019 issue of *Renovatio*, the wonderful journal published by Zaytuna College. It is (hence its relevance here) a meditation on both the unbroken continuity and the continuous brokenness of our "natural" labor to act in accord with our "supernatural" vocation toward transcendental ends—or, rather, on the way in which "natural law" is always subordinate to a supernatural vocation that is at once its foundation and an apocalyptic force that, for spiritual natures, must of necessity subvert it continually.

The fifth essay, "*Geist*'s Kaleidoscope," is something of a complicated case. In its original form, it was written for a *Festschrift* in honor of Cyril O'Regan, one of the great Anglophone Catholic scholars and thinkers of our time, and someone from whom there is always something more to learn, and someone I revere as a friend and as an intellectual force. While both my admiration and my sympathy for O'Regan's project is enormous, this piece does touch upon one of the technical areas where I am in some disagreement with him—the genealogical question, that is, of the "haunted narrative" of German idealism and its relation (which to my mind is nearly nonexistent, in both fact and principle) to ancient "gnosticism." The essay functions here, however, to advance this collection's theme by calling into question a number of conventional theological positions regarding the differences between the Christianity of the New Testament and that of the early "gnostic" schools, as well as certain conventional approaches to the relation between dogmatic tradition and divine revelation. The purpose of doing this, moreover, is not to try to arrive at a particular formulation of the "proper" reading of the theological record, but rather to call attention to a number of contradictions in the conceptual configurations we habitually assume when thinking about the "orthodox" understanding of nature and supernature. It seems clearly to be the case, for instance, that what we think of as the "gnostic" denigration of the created order is an exaggeration of a real "qualified" or "provisional dualism" in the New Testament, and as such is in many ways a more authentic continuation of early Christian understanding of a fallen creation than is, say, the two-tier Thomistic theology of pure nature. According to Christian scripture, we live in the aftermath of an intrinsically divine reality's alienation from its source, not in an order of nature that is the direct work of God's creative will, perfectly innocent in itself, into which we were precipitated from the unnatural "superelevation" accorded us by an extraordinary grace at the inception of humanity's *spiritual* history. At the same time, it seems to me that this gnostic exaggeration of the story of the spiritual fall is the absolute opposite (and certainly not the obscure origin) of those modern theologies that—in appropriating various diluted or simplified forms of German idealist thought—have wanted to see the "alienation" of nature and history as in fact the dialectical achievement of the divine identity. Far from opening the door to "theogonic narratives" analogous to those of German idealism, the early "gnostic" theologies sealed the truly divine off from creation so absolutely as not even to allow room for any true theophany in the material world. And, far from constituting a return of a gnostic impulse, those modern theologies deep-dyed in German idealism represent a final oblivion of precisely that element of "gnostic" suspicion that is closest to the sensibility of the New Testament.

It even seems correct to say that the great failure of the "gnostic" theological imagination is its exaggeration of the estrangement of creation from the truly supernatural (God *in se*)—which results not, mercifully, in a concept of "pure nature," but which does result, every bit as incoherently, in a concept of a reality truly extrinsic and alien to God and therefore beyond all redemption, even through the sorcery of "superelevating grace." At the same time, the great virtue of this vision is that it preserves a proper sense that whatever possesses a supernatural destiny must be supernatural—must be divine—"naturally," while anything truly outside the sphere of this natural divinity (were any such thing possible) could never be joined to God. It is no less correct, however, to say that the great failure of theologies inspired by German idealist tradition is the tendency to understand this primordial inseparability of the "natural" and the "supernatural" in the terms of the former: to confine the supernatural, in fact, to the limits of what is, in some sense, a mere negative capacity of nature and history—the necessary dependency of the divine on the not-divine in order to achieve its full expression and "spiritual" finality. And, conversely, the great virtue of this vision—paradoxically, perhaps—is precisely the same as that of the "gnostic" vision: the recognition that whatsoever enters into the life of the divine must always already have been divine. More to the point, the "gnostic" vision, despite all its limitations, and despite its ontological and metaphysical naïvetés, is nonetheless nearer to the spirit of the New Testament than any theology that would make room for an autonomous sphere of "nature in itself" apart from fallenness, or for "human nature in itself" apart from humanity's *supernatural* ground and ultimate divine vocation; at the same time, it is also nearer to the New Testament than any theology that would turn the fallenness of creation into a moment within the mystery of the divine, or accord it any probationary or dialectical meaning in itself.

The sixth essay, consisting as it does in a series of theses rather than an argument, defies summary here. It is something of a contrapuntal composition, and rather clumsily fugal at that, and the various themes combined within it have appeared and reappeared in my work with some frequency over the years. Here, perhaps, the implications of some of those themes are unfolded more explicitly than has been the case in the past. But I must leave the "essay" (if that is what it is) to speak—or fail to speak—for itself.

A friend has suggested to me that I might have subtitled this collection "Studies in Vedantic Christianity." I have no objection in principle, though I suspect that to have done so would have provoked so much preliminary consternation and suspicion from some readers as to render the essays incapable of having any effect upon them. And, after all, I might just as well have characterized the position defended in these pages as "Neoplatonic Christianity," since that says more or less the same thing. I have refrained from doing that as well, though, chiefly because, to my mind, the phrase constitutes something of a pleonasm. Perhaps, however, it would be best simply to note that—on the question of "grace" and "nature"—these pages advance an Eastern Christian view over against a particular set of Western Christian traditions. Indeed, if there is one thing on which all the great Orthodox theologians of the last century were agreed, despite all their differences from one another, it was that the entire problem of grace and nature (which was known to them almost exclusively from Thomist sources, many of them French) was a false dilemma created by an inept reading of Paul and by a catastrophic division into discrete categories of what should never have been divided. There is only χάρις, which is at once that which is freely given, the delight taken in the gift, and the thanksgiving offered up for it; and all those things that a distorted theology converts into oppositions or dialectical contraries or saltations—grace and nature, creation and deification, nature and supernature—are in fact only differing vantages upon, or continuously varying intensities within, a single transcendent act, a single immanent mystery.

I HAVE PROBABLY SAID ENOUGH. Even so, before parting, I should like to advance five propositions—five premises, really—in part in order to add provocation to provocation, but mostly in order to elucidate the perspective from which this book is written.

1. The sole sufficient natural end of all spiritual creatures is the supernatural, and grace is nothing but the necessary liberation of all creatures for their natural ends.
2. Nature stands in relation to supernature as (in Aristotelian terms) prime matter to form. Nature in itself has no real existence and can have none; it is entirely an ontological patiency before the formal

causality of supernature, and only as grace can nature possess any actuality at all.

3. No spiritual creature could fail to achieve its naturally supernatural end unless God himself were the direct *moral* cause of evil in that creature, which is impossible. Conversely, God saves creatures by removing extrinsic, *physical* (that is, non-moral) impediments to their natural union with him.

4. God became human so that humans should become God. Only the God who is always already human can become human. Only a humanity that is always already divine can become God.

5. God is all that is. Whatever is not God exists as becoming divine, and as such is God in the mode of what is other than God. But God is not "the other" of anything.

ONE

Waking the Gods

Theosis as Reason's Natural End

Τί γὰρ θεώσεως τοῖς ἀξίοις ἐρασμιώτερον, καθ᾽ ἣν ὁ Θεὸς Θεοῖς
γενομένοις ἐνούμενος τὸ πᾶν ἑαυτοῦ ποιεῖται δι᾽ ἀγαθότητα;
Διὸ καὶ ἡδονὴν καὶ πεῖσιν καὶ χαρὰν καλῶς ὠνόμασαν τὴν
τοιαύτην κατάστασιν, τὴν τῇ θείᾳ κατανοήσει καὶ τῇ ἑπομένῃ
αὐτῇ τῆς εὐφροσύνης ἀπολαύσει ἐγγινομένην, ἡδονὴν μέν, ὡς
τέλος οὖσαν τῶν κατὰ φύσιν ἐνεργειῶν (οὕτω γὰρ τὴν ἡδονὴν
ὁρίζονται) . . .

—Maximus the Confessor[1]

I

It is a source of constant vexation to me, as I am sure it must be to all of
us, that philosophical theology pays such scant attention to root vegeta-
bles. Obviously, after so many centuries of appalling neglect, this is not
a deficiency that can be remedied in a day; but, even so, we should not
shirk such small corrective efforts as we are able to undertake. So imagine, if you will, a turnip. Imagine it set before you on a table. But imagine also that, only a few moments ago, it was not a turnip, but a rabbit

instead, and that I have just now magically conjured the one thing out of the other. I do not mean, I hasten to add, that I am an illusionist who has just performed a very clever trick. Rather, mine was a genuine feat of goetic sorcery, probably accomplished with the assistance of a daemon familiar. Contain your wonder. Then tell me: Have I actually transformed a rabbit into a turnip—is that logically possible—or have I instead merely annihilated the poor bunny and then recombined its material ingredients into something else altogether? Surely, it seems obvious, the answer must be the latter. It may well be that precisely the same molecules—even the same atoms—once found in the rabbit are now securely invested in the turnip; but there is nothing leporine remaining in the turnip, and neither was there any trace of rapinity (rapitude?) in the rabbit. I assume that this is uncontroversial. Very well. What, though, if instead I had transformed the rabbit not into another terrestrial organism, especially not one presumably lower in the chain of being, but had instead, so to speak, superelevated it by changing it into a more eminent kind of entity—say, an angel? Much the same question arises: has the rabbit *become* an angel, or has it again merely perished and been replaced by something else? The answer depends, I suppose, on whether one thinks there is already something angelic about rabbits (as I do, but as many do not); for, if there is no latent angelism in rabbits, even of the most purely potential kind, then again no real metamorphosis has occurred at the level of discrete substances or identities. All that has happened is that I have murdered a harmless bunny and summoned up a potentially very dangerous spiritual creature to take its place (one that may not at all approve of my callousness toward small helpless animals).

This is, of course, more or less the opposite of the Ship of Theseus conundrum. The question at issue is not a mereological or metaphysical query about whether a substantial form, individuated by its material instantiation, remains identical with itself as each of its material parts is successively replaced. Rather, it is something more along the lines of asking what continuity exists between, say, a stand of trees and a ship composed from their wood. And it seems obvious that those trees—understood as discrete substances, modes, or just relatively stable objects of deictic reference—have not become a ship, but have instead ceased to exist in order that the ship might come into being. Whatever continuity persists between the trees and the ship is found only in a common substrate, at the level of sheer material plasticity, and is ultimately reducible to that pure indeterminate potency traditionally called prime matter or ὕλη. This alone remains constant across all transformations precisely because it is in itself nothing as such, and so is always absolute: *absolved*, that is, of all formal identity. It can relinquish one form in order to be subsumed into another without being itself altered because in itself it is nothing other than the abiding reality of pure possibility. There is no "thing" to be altered. At the level of actual forms and natures and determinate properties, however, nothing can ever truly become anything other than what it already is, at least potentially. A discrete substance can pass through various states proper to itself, achieve diverse stages of natural development, acquire or shed modalities or accidents implicit in its own nature. But it can never become something truly *extrinsic* to itself without ceasing to be what it was.

If, by the way, I seem to be slipping too easily and unreflectively into an Aristotelian patois, I do so without remorse. For one thing, the particular issues I want to discuss here have traditionally been couched in just such terms. More to the point, though, traditional Aristotelian language concerning the relation between potentiality and actuality seems to me merely to express what I take to be a very basic and logically impeccable modal grammar. Every specific possibility is finite; conversely, infinite possibility can never be specific. And this same elementary logical solvency can be ascribed to the whole Aristotelian language of causality, so long as one does not make the mistake—characteristic of much seventeenth-century science, with its agent and patient substances and forces—of imagining that that language concerns "causes" in the modern sense. Really, a better rendering of *"aitiai"* or *"causae,"* in the ancient or mediaeval acceptation, might be "explanations," "rationales," "logical descriptions," or "rational relations." The fourfold nexus of causality was chiefly a rule of predication, describing the inherent logical structure of anything that exists insofar as it exists, and reflecting a world in which things and events are at once discretely identifiable and yet part of the continuum of the whole. A thing's *aitiai* are intrinsic integral logical relations, not separated forces in only accidental alliance. A final cause is the inherent natural limit of a particular possibility, not an extrinsically imposed design; it is at once a thing's intrinsic fullness and its larger participation in the totality of nature. So a causal relation in this scheme is less like a physical exchange of energy than like a mathematical equation, and the final cause is like the inevitable sum determining that relation. And the logic of finality, if one grants it (as one must), tells us that the only substantial transformations that are not essentially annihilations are modifications already virtually embraced within the natural potentials of the thing transformed. There may be differing modes of leporinity, for instance, and any number of possible accidents thereof, but none of these is the condition of being a turnip. A rabbit cannot be—and therefore cannot become—a turnip, any more than a circle can be—or can become—a square.

II

Why is any of this important here? Principally for historical reasons. It is very easy to forget, after all, that many of the most important theological developments and movements in both Roman Catholic and Eastern Orthodox theology in the first half of the twentieth century—*ressourcement*, *la nouvelle théologie*, the neopatristic synthesis, Neopalamism, even certain salient aspects of Bulgakov's mature thought—took shape in the same, largely Parisian intellectual atmosphere, and defined themselves to a significant degree over against what was then the dominant theology of grace in Roman Catholic thought: that of the Baroque "manualist" Thomism whose institutional cry of triumph had rung out so stridently in 1879's encyclical *Aeterni Patris* but had already diminished to an asperous death rattle by the time of 1950's *Humani generis*. This was the infamous "two-tier" Thomism—or so its detractors called it—that had had no real antecedents in theological tradition much before the *de auxiliis* controversy of the sixteenth century, that had achieved preeminence only in the days of the "modernist crisis," that was already on the way to its well-deserved demise with the publication of Maurice Blondel's *L'action* in 1893, and did not long survive Henri de Lubac's *Surnaturel* in 1946. And, until very recently, most of us thought it had been laid permanently to rest, in the deepest, dankest, and most dismal of theology's unvisited crypts. Apparently, however, someone neglected to drive a stake through its heart and cut off its head, because in the last two decades it has enjoyed a surprisingly robust reviviscence in some of the more militantly necrophile factions of traditionalist Catholicism. And so, now that the damned monster is up from its grave and spasmodically lurching about again, spreading terror among the villagers and hill-folk, this might be a propitious time for Orthodox theologians to reconsider what was learned (or should have been learned) in those earlier encounters with it. (Who knows but that it will ultimately be up to them to save the occidental barbarians from themselves?)

From an Eastern perspective, the debate on the "supernatural"—epochal though it was for Catholic theology—can only seem a bit bizarre. What had become the "Thomist" position (which must be distinguished, incidentally, from any position we can confidently attribute to Thomas himself) was that a proper appreciation of the gratuity of salvation and deification can be secured only by insisting that, as the tedious formula goes, "grace is extrinsic to the nature of the creature." That is to say, human nature has no inherent ordination toward real union with God, and—apart from the infusion of a certain wholly adventitious *lumen gloriae*—rational creatures are incapable even of conceiving a desire for such union. Even the unremitting agitations of Augustine's *cor inquietum* are superadded spiritual motives that, in the current providential order of this world, happen to have been graciously conjoined to the natural intentionalities of created rational wills. But, so the claim goes, none of that need be the case. God could just as well have created a world in a state of *natura pura*, wherein the rational volitions of spiritual creatures could have achieved all their final ends and ultimate rest in an entirely natural terminus. The only longing for God such creatures would naturally experience would be an elicited velleity or abstract curiosity obscurely directed toward some original explanatory principle that might tell them where the world came from. Or, in some cases, for those who may have heard of the possibility of the beatific vision in the abstract, there might be an elicited "conditional" desire to see what it is like; but this would still not be the kind of supernatural appetite and superadded capacity that efficacious grace alone can infuse in a soul. And, even then, those ungraced spirits need never discover that principle or that possible end *in itself* in order to be wholly satisfied in their rational longings, since God thus "naturally" conceived remains the object of an only incidental inquisitiveness, adequately known in and through creatures. Moreover, supposedly, even in *this* world, where rational natures do bear the gracious imprint of a vocation to deification, human nature in itself remains entirely identical to what human nature would have been in a world without grace. Nature *as such* has no claim on grace, even where such grace is given, nor does it even have any awareness that such grace is desirable *unless* that grace is actually given. Hence the term "two-tier" Thomism: Nature is a circumscribed totality, a self-sufficient *suppositum*, while grace is a *superadditum* set, as it were, atop it, and only thereby superelevating nature beyond itself. And here too one sees the effect of a certain Thomist tendency to see the Fall as humanity's descent from a graciously elevated state (Eden) into the state of nature as God had created it in its integrity (including such essential features as suffering and death), as opposed to the Christian view that the Fall was the descent of humanity and the whole cosmos from their original and natural condition into an unnatural state of bondage to decay (including such accidental features as suffering and death).

Now, clearly, the two-tier picture is alien to the whole of patristic tradition—indeed, more or less antithetical to it—and probably, I think, to most or all of mediaeval tradition. Its rise in early modernity was the result of an accident of theological history. Thomas himself in many places, and most insistently in the *Summa contra gentiles*, asserts that "*omnis intellectus naturaliter desiderat divinae substantiae visionem*," "every intellect naturally desires the vision of the divine nature";[2] and that no finite intelligible object is sufficient for human happiness because the only final end of natural human desire is the real knowledge of God;[3] and that rational mind is created specifically for the purpose of seeing God.[4] It is something of a refrain in his writings.[5] But, on the threshold of modernity, these claims became suspect, as they seemed to fall afoul of the Aristotelian principle—or, at least, of an inexplicably fashionable exaggeration of the Aristotelian principle—that, as Denis the Carthusian (1402–71) puts it, "no natural desire can exceed natural capacity":[6] an axiom hazily drawn from Aristotle's claim in *De caelo* (where it functions not really so much as a logical assertion as a "providential" maxim) that "had Nature endowed celestial bodies with an inclination to linear movement, she would have supplied the means for it as well."[7] There is, admittedly, a banal truism here, since a "natural" desire is necessarily determined toward a specific final cause; but how this should apply to the very special case of rational spirit is precisely the issue that the later Thomist tradition could not coherently answer because it was inhibited by its commitment to a very particular understanding of grace. Cajetan (1469–1534), for instance, took it as established that, for any rational creature, "*naturale eius desiderium non se extendit ultra facultatem,*" "its natural desire cannot extend beyond its own faculty,"[8] and that therefore created intellect does not naturally desire God *in se*; for it cannot aspire to an object to which the "*tota vis naturae,*" "the whole power of nature," is inadequate.[9] Therefore, supposedly, it must be the case that when Thomas speaks of the natural desire for God he is referring solely to the present providential order, in which human nature has already received grace's extrinsic mark. But then, even within this order, we must still acknowledge two distinct finalities for human beings: the "supposited" natural end and the graciously "superposited" supernatural end. The "first gift" of creation and the "second gift" of deification belong to two discontinuous moments of divine largesse.

I am indifferent to whether this is the correct reading of Thomas.[10] I do, though, think it worthwhile to make a few obvious points. For one thing, as I am hardly the first to note, the principle of proportionality between natural desire and desire's ends ought not to be mistaken for a rule regarding the range of a creature's innate spontaneous powers. What is *natural* for us is not necessarily, by that token, something that we are capable of achieving for ourselves. Indeed, insofar as we are finite and contingent beings, everything "natural" about us—the very possession of any nature at all, in fact—is dependent upon some other source or power not only for its realization, but for its very existence. Thomas, for instance, drawing on Aristotle's *Nicomachean Ethics*, plainly states that certain natural inclinations can be fulfilled only through the aid of another, and that there is even a peculiar and superior nobility in those aspects of our nature that require the assistance of friends to bring them to fruition.[11] But, really, are such properties even very rare or exceptional in finite natures? Even Aristotle's celestial bodies, for instance, perpetually enact the cyclophoria of the heavens only because they are drawn ever onward from beyond themselves by the Prime Mover, to which they will never attain. In a sense, almost every natural desire—even, say, for food or for sex—is dependent for its realization on something imparted to it from beyond itself. Even those possibilities most constitutive of us as the finite beings that we are can be fulfilled only in and through the *grace* of cooperating external causes. It was perfectly natural to me, for instance, as an adult human male, to become both a husband and a father. In a sense, the fullness of my humanity—at least, as the person I happen to be—required no less of me. But I was utterly incapable of achieving that natural end without the assistance of at least two other persons. A final cause must be logically implicit in the potency it actuates, true, but not necessarily as some wholly inherent and autonomous power of expression. And there is no logical reason to claim that an end that can be achieved only by *supernatural* assistance is not, for that reason, a *natural* possibility. Indeed, if this were the case, the very concept of natural potential would be meaningless, since any finite reality's very existence is always already a possibility that has been enacted by a wholly supernatural gift of being. A potency can be thoroughly natural in itself even if proportioned to an end that the "whole power of nature" (as we know it, at least) cannot supply. There is no contradiction here. There would be a contradiction only if there were no reality at all corresponding to that natural potency, and so no real final cause implicit in it.

On the other hand—and this again brings us back to the difference between the traditional Thomistic understanding of fallenness (as a descent from a state of gracious exception from nature into one of "natural" mortality and ignorance) and the Christian view (a descent from a natural state of grace into one of unnatural corruption)—why should one assume that a wholly natural (which is also to say, wholly supernatural) progress into deification lies beyond the capacity of an unfallen rational creature?[12] Why would one imagine that the capacity for the desire to see God is not also, apart from the unnatural limitations of sin and death, the natural capacity to achieve deification? Especially if one does not make the error of thinking that such an achievement must be *either* a work of grace *or* a work of nature, but realizes instead that such a distinction is a phantom of fallen consciousness? Even in this life, after all, something of the experience of real divinizing union with God can be vouchsafed to those who are devoted to the spiritual life—ἕνωσις, *unio mystica*, *turiya*, *fanaa-fillah*—and this evidently, however much a gift of grace, is also a real capacity of human nature when that nature is set free from the constraints of an unnatural limitation of consciousness. Every rational nature is already potentially infinite in its embrace of the divine nature, even if that potency can be actualized only as a kind of infinite *epektasis*.

In truth, this entire issue seems to pose a problem only if one is intent on maintaining precisely the kind of impermeable partition between nature and grace that a belief in *creatio ex nihilo* renders meaningless. Grace, to be grace, does not require a prior antithetical *suppositum* of something devoid of grace—pure nature or nature in itself—nor need it be a purely extrinsic gift at every level of its impartation; it need only be free in its entirety. Finite existence itself is always already nothing but the gracious effect of God calling creatures to himself out of nothingness. All those boring false dilemmas bedeviling Western theology since the Pelagian controversy—the causal priority we assign *either* to our own working out of salvation *or* to God working in us, *either* to God's foreknowledge *or* to his sovereignty in election, *either* to the creature's merit *or* to God's, and so on—are simple category errors. Between the immanent and the transcendent, or the finite and the infinite, such rivalries of agency are not even cogently conceivable. An intrinsic rational desire for God would constitute a "right" to God's grace only if our nature were our own achievement. Yes, in a sense God does manifestly owe his creatures grace, within the terms of the gift of creation; but that is a debt he owes ultimately only to his own goodness.

None of that, however, is my principal argument here. I have two very different concerns: one logical (and metaphysical), regarding potentiality and actuality, the other phenomenological (and metaphysical), regarding the necessary structure of rational volition.

III

As to the former, the issue is that same simple, irresoluble logical impasse with which I began these reflections. The traditionalist Thomist answer to the conundrum of how, according to its scheme, grace can be said to perfect rather than abolish human nature—how, that is, a rational creature can be transformed beyond its every intrinsic potency and given a final end wholly extrinsic to its own nature without thereby ceasing to be the creature it has hitherto been—is to assert that our nature's capacity for grace consists in a mere *potentia obœdientialis*. But this can be true only if such a potency is understood in an especially eccentric way: as, that is, a kind of indeterminate ontological plasticity, open to whatever is not repugnant to the creature's nature, and yet also somehow open to actualities genuinely extrinsic to that nature. Supposedly, this pure patiency constitutes a structural aptitude in us for grace that is, nevertheless, in no sense an inchoate possession of grace or an intrinsic disposition toward a supernatural end. This is gibberish. Far from explaining how the interval between grace and nature posited by Thomist tradition can be intelligibly closed without violence to either side of the divide, it is merely a desperate resort to the fantastic. Here we need to distinguish with absolute logical precision between, on the one hand, the potencies proper to a creature's nature and, on the other, whatever powers the creature might individually possess for making those potencies actual. Simply said, whatever is not repugnant to a finite nature is, by definition, an intrinsic possibility of that nature. If divinity is "compatible" with the humanity of a creature made in God's image, then divinity is itself an inherent possibility of humanity—an inherent *property*, in fact, even if in only potential form. That this possibility can become an actuality only by way of God's action toward the creature in no way diminishes or qualifies this truth. Before Cajetan, in fact, obediential potency was understood simply as the creature's predisposition to miraculous interventions from God, and explicitly as a predisposition that in no way violated that creature's native potencies; it referred, that is, to the capacity of any creature to be conduced by God's power to a state that is proper to its own nature but that, in the natural course of things, it could not at that particular juncture achieve on its own. For instance, God could make an old man young again without violation of his nature as a man, as youth is a natural condition for human beings, even if it is not something a man can recover by his own power once it has passed. God could make Sarah bear a child well past her fertile years without in any way imposing upon her a state repugnant to her womanhood. God might make a fool wise without violence to that person's humanity, for wisdom is a natural possible state for a rational being. What the concept of obediential potential most definitely was not, however, was some hazy notion of a mysterious capacity within a creature simultaneously to remain what it is and yet also to become something truly other than itself, or to receive a nature other than its own without thereby losing its own nature. It was not, that is to say, a principle of sorcery or an abrogation of the rule of noncontradiction.[13]

Again, there is an inviolable modal grammar here that must be observed. There are only two kinds of logically conceivable potency: either the finite (formal) possibility of something in particular or the infinite (material) possibility of everything in general. In the former case, a potency is a specific predisposition to and capacity for a particular final end, and so that end necessarily determines that potency's logical structure, and is already implicit in it as a real rational relation; a natural capacity for the supernatural, if conceived thus, would have to be a virtual indwelling of the supernatural in the natural. In the latter case, the potency in question is just pure possibility as such, *materia prima* as it were, intrinsically disposed to no particular end, absolved of all determinacy, persisting despite the displacement of one form by another precisely because it lacks the power to retain any formal determination in itself and so is able to relinquish one nature in order to assume another; a natural capacity for the supernatural, if conceived thus, would be impotent to preserve the form or nature it inhabits in receiving an extrinsic determination, just as the material substrate of a tree would be impotent to preserve a tree's form or nature in being subsumed into a ship. In either case, whatever is *wholly* extrinsic to the creature's nature must remain extrinsic forever. And this impasse cannot be resolved by the introduction of some chimerical *tertium quid* that is neither one kind of possibility nor the other, but rather some obscure amalgamation of the two. To invoke an "obediential potential" here is to play the sorcerer's apprentice—to recite a spell in the hope that something extraordinary will appear and magically perform a task for us that we cannot accomplish for ourselves. Once again, we can become only what we are.[14] And so, if we do possess a natural desire for the supernatural, it cannot be a mere contingency of providence, superadded to our nature; the potential of *theosis* must always already be the very structure of our nature in any possible order of reality. And, as it happens, we do possess such a desire, and could not fail to do so without entirely ceasing to be rational agents.

Not that this has always been fully appreciated, even by committed opponents of the two-tier system. Even many of de Lubac's defenders seem willing to concede a modified version of the *natura pura* argument. David Braine, for instance, while rejecting the notion that there is such a thing as human nature in the abstract that would be the same reality either with or without the supplement of a supernatural vocation to union with God, still allowed for the possibility that, under the conditions of some other created dispensation, God could create a different but still rational human nature not bearing the imprint of a supernatural finality; for him, it was enough to assert that human nature as it actually exists in the present order of providence, instantiated solely in the concrete historical community of the first and last Adams, simply happens to include that finality as an objective and given fact about the world that God chose to create.[15] And de Lubac himself, after the 1950 promulgation of *Humani generis*, professed perfect agreement with the encyclical—and this despite the document's condemnation of the proposition that God "cannot create intellectual beings without calling and ordering them to the beatific vision." By 1965, he was arguing vigorously for a stark distinction between the first gift of creation and the second gift of the vocation to deification.[16] By the end, the only clear difference from the manualist orthodoxy in his stated opinion was a preference for speaking not of two distinct *final* ends, but rather of one end that is only *penultimate* and another that is alone truly *ultimate*. Whether this was truly his position in 1946, when *Surnaturel* was published, I cannot say, though I doubt it;[17] I suspect he stated his real view, in its purest form, in a letter of 3 April 1932 to Maurice Blondel: "How can a conscious spirit be anything other than an absolute desire for God?"[18] If, though, he truly concurred with the encyclical, so much the worse for him; because the principle that Piux XII was so eager to reject in those pages happens to be an analytic truth of reason, no more susceptible of doubt than is the principle of identity. Not even God could create a rational nature not called to deification, any more than he could create a square circle; to have received that call is precisely what it is to be a rational being. In fact, I would go so far as to say that a spiritual creature can possess no *purely* natural end at all, not even as a penultimate station along the way, and certainly none to which a supernatural end is merely contingently or gratuitously superadded. Quite the contrary: a spiritual creature is capable of a rational desire for a natural end only within the embrace of a prior supernatural longing, and hence a spiritual creature appropriates any given natural good not merely as an end in itself, but as more originally an expression of the supernatural Good. A finite intention of intellect and will is possible only as the effect of a prior infinite intentionality. Any intellectual predilection toward a merely immediate terminus of longing can be nothing other than a mediating modality and local contraction of a total spiritual volition toward the divine. One cannot contemplate a flower, watch a play, or pluck a strawberry from a punnet without being situated within an irrefrangible intentional continuum that extends all the way to God in his fullness.[19]

This may seem an extravagant claim, but its denial is something worse. The very notion that a rational spiritual creature could conceivably inhabit a realm of pure nature, in which it could rest satisfied and in which its only intellectual concern regarding God would consist in a purely speculative, purely aetiological curiosity *posteriorly* elicited from finite cognitions, is a logical nonsense. Those finite cognitions, to the degree they could be comprehended and then interpreted as implying further logical entailments, would have to be acts of intentionality and rational evaluation undertaken in light of an intelligibility supplied by the mind's prior preoccupation with wholly transcendental indices of meaning, and so would also have to be a proleptic intentional awareness of and desire for the supernatural *in its essence* as an *intelligibile*. Neither doctrine nor metaphysics need be immediately invoked to see the impossibility of rational agency within a sphere of pure nature; a simple phenomenology of what it is we do when we act intentionally should suffice. The rational will, when freely moved, is always purposive; it acts always toward an end: conceived, perceived, imagined, hoped for, resolved upon. Its every movement is already, necessarily, an act of recognition, judgment, evaluation, and decision, and is therefore also a tacit or explicit reference to a larger, more transcendent realm of values, meanings, and rational longings. Desire and knowledge are always, in a single impulse, directed to some purpose present to the mind, even if only vaguely. Any act lacking such purposiveness is by definition not an act of rational freedom. There are, moreover, only two possible ways of pursuing a purpose: either as an end in itself or as a provisional end pursued for the sake of an end beyond itself. But no finite object or purpose can wholly attract the rational will in the latter way, and no finite thing is desirable in the former. A finite object may, in relative terms, constitute a more compelling end that makes a less compelling end nonetheless instrumentally desirable, but it can never constitute an end *in itself*. It too requires an end beyond itself to be compelling in any measure; it too can evoke desire only on account of some yet higher, more primordial, more general disposition of reason's appetites. If not for some always more original orientation toward an always more final end, the will would never act in regard to finite objects at all. Even what pleases us most immediately can be intentionally desired only within the context of a rational longing for the Good in its own fullness. Immanent desires are always at a higher level deferred toward some more remote, more transcendent purpose. All concretely limited aspirations of the will are sustained within formally limitless aspirations of the will. In the end, the only objects of desire that are not reducible to other, more general objects of desire, and that are thus desirable entirely in and of themselves, are those universal, unconditional, and exalted ideals, those transcendentals, that constitute being's abstract perfections. One may not be, in any given instant, immediately conscious that one's rational appetites have been excited by these transcendental ends; I am not talking about a psychological state of the empirical ego; but those ends are the constant and pervasive preoccupation of the rational will in the deepest springs of its nature, the source of that "delectable perturbation"[20] that grants us a conceptual grasp of finite realities precisely by carrying us restlessly beyond them and thereby denying them even a provisional ultimacy.

The truth is—and, again, this is a purely phenomenological observation—we cannot possess so much as the barest rational cognizance of the world we inhabit except insofar as we have always already, in our rational intentions, exceeded the world. Intentional recognition is always already interpretation, and interpretation is always already judgment. The intellect is not a passive mirror reflecting a reality that simply composes itself for us within our experience; rather, intellect is itself an agency that converts the storm of sense-intuitions into a comprehensible order through a constant process of construal. And it is able to do this by virtue of its always more original, tacit recognition of an object of rational longing—say, Truth itself—that appears nowhere within the natural order, but toward which the mind nevertheless naturally reaches out, as to its only possible place of final rest. All proximate objects are known to us, and so desired or disregarded or rejected, in light of that anticipated finality. Even to seek to know, to organize experience into reflection, is a venture of the reasoning will toward that absolute horizon of intelligibility. And since truly rational desire can never be a purely spontaneous eruption of the will without purpose, it must exhibit its final cause in the transcendental structure of its operation. Rational experience, from the first, is a movement of rapture, of ecstasy toward ends that must be understood as—because they must necessarily be desired as—nothing less than the perfections of being, ultimately convertible with one another in the fullness of reality's one source and end. Thus the world as something available to our intentionality comes to us in the interval that lies between the mind's indivisible unity of apprehension and the irreducibly transcendental horizon of its intention—between, that is, the first cause of movement in the mind and the mind's natural telos, both of which lie outside the composite totality of nature. And so the rational will's absolute preoccupation with being as a whole discloses the rather astonishing truth that the very structure of all intellection is an essential relation to God's transcendence as spirit's only possible *natural* end. As I say, for spiritual creatures, nature is experienced *as* nature only by way of a more original apprehension of the supernatural. These transcendental ends are ultimate objects of desire, after all, only in that God's transcendent goodness shines through them; and reason must love the Good.

Neither, incidentally, can that transcendental horizon be an only natural terminus of mind and will, consisting in *created* objects of rational longing, *transcendentalia ordinata* (as it were) forming merely the most remote and exalted reaches of the realm of pure nature.[21] Such a notion invites only an infinite regress of final causalities, since a purely ordained object of desire still could not attract a rational nature except as illuminated by a yet more eminent end, desirable in itself. A transcendental terminus of rational yearning has its power to attract the intellect only as the splendor of God's goodness, truth, beauty, and simplicity. To desire to know the truth, for instance, is to desire that everything opaque to the understanding in experience—everything that might defy thought's overtures and importunities—progressively vanish, until mind and world together achieve perfect transparency one to the other. The mind longs from the first not only to reach, but to *become*, that divine truth that gives being to all things. It seeks, as Maximus the Confessor says, to pass beyond all finite cognitions and enter at last into a final union with its first causes in God.[22] Rational spirit, teleologically specified, *is* God; that is its horizon of final causality, because the end it seeks is the knowledge of all things in God's perfect act of knowledge, the ultimate transparency of our *scientia vespertina* to his infinite *scientia matutina*. And, again, a final cause is always a real rational relation within—and so is constitutive of—whatever efficient movement it draws into actuality. Conversely, the mind can only be moved by what is in some sense possible for it, at the very least as a rational desire. Reduced to its most primal origin and ultimate end, then—to what precedes and surpasses the empirical world, what founds and elicits the whole movement of thought in which the phenomenal world subsists—rational life is a finite participation in an infinite act of thought that is also the whole of being: the simplicity of God knowing God. And so the basis of all knowledge and intentional will is the natural desire of the creature for *theosis*.

I should add here, moreover, two observations. The first is that these considerations make it obvious that any meaningful distinction between the natural desire for God as the "best intelligible object" and the supernatural desire to "see him as he is" can be no more than a distinction, within a single continuous order of desire, between an imperfect and a perfect apprehension of the same end; and the latter end is the necessary condition of the former, and most definitely not something superadded thereto. We cannot desire the best intelligible object without first and more comprehensively and more ultimately desiring the fullness of both intelligibility as such and excellence as such. I mention this because, again, much Thomist tradition inserts the division of its incommiscible tiers at precisely this juncture in the *ordo cognoscendi*, and in so doing reduces both *termini* of rational longing—God as the ultimate object of natural curiosity, God in himself as the end of supernatural desire—into arbitrary and discontinuous objects of will, apart from every intrinsically coherent rationale. The natural desire to know, thus conceived, would have no proper transcendental motive to explain it, while supernatural desire would be a bizarre saltation beyond all creaturely integrity, one that would not perfect nature, but would instead actually erase it. This way of seeing matters disrupts the rational continuum between natural and supernatural longing quite beyond repair. In order to long for the best possible intelligible object—and thereby the ultimate explanatory principle of nature—one must first be moved by the desire for (and hence proleptic knowledge of) the direct vision of truth in itself as that which is most high: God "as he is." God (even as a mere "explanatory principle") could never be an object of natural desire if there were not already on the creature's part a more primordial consuming longing for, and constant supernatural awareness of, the knowledge of God in himself in the light of glory. And here one must assume that Thomas himself was unable to resolve the ambiguity in some of his own language. When, for instance, he considers the issue of whether the angels were created in a state of perfect beatitude, and whether then they fell from a condition of supernatural grace,[23] he is obliged to assert that they were created at first only in the state of natural beatitude, capable of perceiving God only under the conditions of their evening knowledge, knowing the Word by the similitude thereof shining forth in their own created nature, but not yet knowing the Word in the full light of glory.[24] But Thomas also knows that, if this glorious morning knowledge truly perfects the evening knowledge conferred by nature, then the latter must be intrinsically ordained to the former.[25] Yet there could be no such ordination were the latter not already the premise of the former in the real order of rational desire, as an end implicit in every movement of spirit toward any object. Nothing can be ordained to an end not intrinsic to its nature, and no natural end can attract a spiritual nature except insofar as it is perceived as illuminated by the ultimate index of rational desirability. There is no natural light apart from the prior illumination of the light of glory.

And the second observation is, in keeping with the logic of act and potency unfolded above, that I do not believe that phenomenology can be sealed off from metaphysics. I do not believe in the possibility of that kind of *epochē*. To acknowledge the transcendent end presupposed by all acts of rational will is to assert also the reality of that final cause as the only possible explanation for the reality of rational existence. But for that abiding and real harmony of knowing and being, that perfect coincidence of spiritual longing and its end in the real final cause (God in himself), rational existence would be an *ontological* impossibility. It certainly could not come about as the emergent result of some inchoate striving of the will prior to the reality it posits for itself, as any such striving would always be reducible to an infinite regress, one irrational spontaneity after another without end. A metaphysical deduction alone can account for what a phenomenological reduction discloses. That final horizon of desire is a real rational relation within the structure of that desire; and a real rational relation is, of necessity, a real ontological cause (or, better, *aitia*). To recognize the shape of rational desire, then, is to acknowledge the real indwelling within rational spirit of a final cause that is nothing less than intrinsically divine.

IV

I should add also that I do not believe that, for Christians, these issues can be decided without reference to what revelation requires them to affirm. And, as it happens, if one were to consider these issues purely theologically, one's deepest dissatisfaction with the traditionalist Thomist view might well follow not from any particular act of phenomenological reduction, but out of solicitude for the theology of the incarnation. Orthodox Christology, after all, insists not merely that there is no conflict or rivalry between Christ's divinity and his humanity, nor merely that they are capable of harmonious accord with one another. Rather, it asserts that humanity is so naturally compatible with divinity that the Son can be both fully divine and fully human at once without separation or confusion, in one agent whose actions are all therefore at once fully human and fully divine. If our nature were not already wholly contained within the divine, and the divine not already innate in us, then the incarnation of the Son would have to be an extrinsic juxtaposition of natures "reconciled" with one another, either by a kind of miraculous occasionalism or else by way of a real change in both natures, producing a fusion or synthesis that would supplant the divine and the human alike with a new reality essentially different from both at once. But then Christ would be not the God-man, but rather a semi-divine monstrosity: either a divine-human chimaera or a divine-human hybrid. Once again, we cannot escape this problem by resorting to the vague, meaningless, modally amphibologous mechanism of the *potentia obœdientialis* (in its distorted form). And, really, why should we want to do so? Do we truly wish to imagine that what the incarnation of the Logos revealed was not, at the very last, the deepest truth of rational nature, but rather only the accidental fact of a superadded impress upon that nature as vouchsafed within one particular contingent order of providence? Or that deification in Christ is the consummation not of the eternal truth of rational natures but only of one possible but logically fortuitous fate for such natures? Even if I did not regard this picture as logically incoherent, I should still find it theologically repellant.

At any rate, if nothing else, it seems clear to me that the early modern Thomist synthesis was the product of a long history of illusory dilemmas generated by false dichotomies. All too often, the debate was shaped by perceived antitheses and disjunctions where there were in reality only continuities, albeit as descried from sometimes inverse perspectives. Just as the *ordo cognoscendi* and the *ordo essendi* are one and the same continuum (as considered now from one pole, now from the other), so too perhaps are such seeming binary oppositions as nature and grace, creation and deification, the first gift and the second gift, the claims of the creature upon God and God's gifts to the creature—not to mention sufficient and efficacious grace, or the antecedent and consequent decrees of God, or any number of other oppositions that this essay has not directly addressed. And the passage from one pole to the other, rather than involving an extrinsic addition to or intrinsic annihilation of anything, should be understood as occurring only along that continuum, and as progressing only by relative degrees of intensity within an original unity. There is no abiding difference within the one gift of both creation and deification; there is only grace all the way down and nature all the way up, and "pure nature"—like pure potency or pure nothingness—is a remainder concept of the most vacuous kind: the name of something that in itself could never be anything at all. Creation, incarnation, salvation, deification: in God, these are one gracious act, one absolute divine vocation to the creature to become what he has called it to become.[26]

I should note, by the way, that I do accept some version of a principle of proportion between natural desires and their final ends; but the conclusion I draw from this principle is quite the opposite of the one reached by traditional Thomism. I take it to imply that the natural capacity of rational creatures—though it is a capacity that can be satisfied only through the aid of another—is formally and teleologically infinite.[27] Thus, as Nicholas of Cusa so acutely notes, the natural desire of spiritual creatures is ultimately oriented to God not as some kind of comprehensible quiddity, but solely as the incomprehensible infinite.[28] By its very nature, spiritual desire can never be formally teleologically finite, as the finite cannot be its own index of rational desirability. As Nicholas says, *"Quod nisi deus esset infinitus, non foret finis desidere"*:[29] "Were God not infinite, he would not be the end for desire." The natural desire of spiritual creatures is nothing less, in its fullness, than an infinite intention corresponding to an infinite gift. That certainly was the conviction of Gregory of Nyssa, who would never have guessed that grace and nature might be conceived of as two opposed categories, who believed instead that human nature in its very essence is meant to become an ever more radiant mirror of the divine beauty and ever fuller intimacy of the divine presence, and whom I tend to trust more than just about any other theologian on these matters. From eternity, God has brought spiritual creatures into existence in the only way that such creatures could be formed: by calling them to ascend out of the darkness of nonbeing into the infinite beauty of the divine nature. To exist as a spiritual creature is simply to have heard and (from the very first instant) responded to this total vocation. Creation is already deification—is, in fact, theogony. For that eternal act—that summoning of all created natures out of the primordial darkness—is most certainly an entirely free and unmerited gift of being, imparted to those who were not and who in themselves had no claim to be; but it is also, and no less originally, the call that awakens the gods.

TWO

The Treasure of Delight

Nicholas of Cusa on Infinite Desire

I

In one of the earlier passages in his *Zibaldone*,[1] Leopardi reflects at considerable length upon what he takes to be a sentiment common to all of us: a sense he believes we all share of the "*nullità di tutte le cose*," "the nullity of everything," the insufficiency of every pleasure to satisfy the spirit within us, and "*la tendenza nostra verso un infinito che non comprendiamo*," "our inclination toward an infinite that we do not comprehend." It is, taken as a whole, a *tour de force* of psychological phenomenology. It also, however, begins from a logical error; for, according to Leopardi, both this persistent dissatisfaction within us and the infinity of longing that underlie it can probably be ascribed to a cause "*più materiale che spirituale*," "more material than spiritual." Which is to say, he begins by assuming a contradiction: that an infinite intention, exceeding every finite object of rational longing, could arise spontaneously from finite physical causes, without any transcendental end to provoke it as, at least, an intentional object and capacity of the rational will. But how, then, could we experience this *tendenza* at all as an actual intelligible volition beyond what lies immediately before us, and arrive at an awareness that it is unfulfilled? An intention without a final intentional horizon can be experienced neither as fulfilled nor as unfulfilled. And yet Leopardi recognizes that our desire for pleasure is limitless in duration and extent, and that we would not exist as the beings we are without it; it belongs to our substance, he says, not as a longing for this or that, but as a desire for the pleasing as such. And here he is quite correct. One can desire nothing finite as an end wholly in itself, but only "*come piacere astratto e illimitato*,"[2] "as abstract and limitless pleasure." "*Conseguito un piacere, l'anima non cessa di desiderare il piacere, come non cessa mai di pensare, perchè il pensiero e il desiderio del piacere sono due operazioni egualmente continue e inseparabili dalla sua esistenza*":[3] "Following on one pleasure, the soul does not cease from desire for pleasure, just as it never ceases thinking, because thought and desire for pleasure are two operations equally continuous with and inseparable from our existence." Indeed. But, then, what Leopardi's reflections actually reveal is that our ability to desire anything as a purpose conceived by the willing mind is inexplicable unless we presume that the source of that desire is a transcendental object (real or supposed) to which our rational wills are—at least, again, intentionally—wholly adequate. As a matter of simple fact, all purposive human desire is animated at its most primordial level by an unremitting volition toward (for want of a better term) the divine. *Cor nostrum inquietum est donec requiescat in te*, to coin a phrase.

One can see, of course, why as unremittingly dour a godless genius as Leopardi would not be inclined to follow his musings to the conclusion they appear to entail. To grant that the human spirit is capable of a genuinely infinite intentionality is already to grant that the sort of bleak materialism he presumed is at best paradoxical, at worst incoherent. If nothing else, it would mean that even that aspect of human character that seems most irrational—our inability to rest finally content in any proximate and finite end of longing—is in fact the result of a prior and wholly rational relation between human spirit and the proper end of rational freedom as such. That irrepressible disquiet is not merely the insatiable perversity of aimless appetite, magically positing an ever more exalted end for itself somewhere out there in the nowhere of the will's spontaneous energies, but is rather a constant and cogent longing that apprises us of the true ultimate rationale that prompts the mind and will to seek any end at all, and therefore to be capable of recognition, evaluation, judgment, and choice in regard to proximate ends: a rationale that lies elsewhere, beyond the limits of the finite. This also, moreover, touches upon a very old issue within the history of Western metaphysics: the gradual discovery that infinity is not merely a name for unintelligible indeterminate extension—as was the prejudice of early Platonic, Aristotelian, and Stoic thought—nor even merely a positive rational category; rather, infinity is also a proper name for that *necessary* terminus of all real rational freedom apart from which neither reason nor freedom could exist. Plotinus is perhaps the first Western thinker to have grasped this explicitly. In Christian thought, it was Gregory of Nyssa who first unfolded the principle at length, and with consummate brilliance. But no Christian figure after Gregory, with the possible exception of Maurice Blondel, grasped the principle in all its dimensions as fully as did Nicholas of Cusa. As he writes in *De visione dei*, "*Quod nisi deus esset infinitus, non foret finis desidere*": "Were God not infinite, he could not be the end for desire."[4] To which, of course, corresponds the reciprocal proposition that nothing desired as a limited quiddity, without any remainder of the "ever greater," can be in itself the sole final cause prompting that desire.[5]

Actually, the sixteenth chapter of *De visione*[6] is oddly similar in some ways to that passage from Leopardi cited above, though of course radically different in intonation. You, God, says Nicholas, "*es forma omnis desiderabilis et veritas illa quae in omni desiderio desideratur*": "are the form of every desirable thing and are that truth that is desired within every desire"; "*degustare incomprehensibilem suavitatem tuam, quae tanto mihi fit gratior quanto infinitior apparet*," "to taste of your incomprehensible sweetness, which becomes more delightful to me to the very degree that it seems more infinite," is to see that, precisely because the divine is ultimately unknown to all creatures, "*habeant in sacratissima ignorantia maiorem quietum, quasi in thesauro innumerabili et inexhaustibili*," "they might in holiest ignorance possess a greater contentment, as though amid an incalculable and inexhaustible treasure." Hence, the creature's ignorance of God's full greatness is a "*pascentia . . . desiderabilissima*," a "supremely desirable feasting," for the intellect.[7] And hence, also, it is God's will both "*comprehendi possessione mea et manere incomprehensibilis et infinitus*," "to be comprehended in my possession and also to remain incomprehensible and infinite," because he is a treasure whose end no one can desire. Neither can this rational appetite desire the cessation of its own existence. The *will* may long either to exist or not to exist, but appetite itself cannot desist from itself, for it "*fertur in infinitum*," "is borne into the infinite." "*Desiderium enim intellectuale non fertur in id quod potest esse maius et desiderabilius, sed in id quod non potest maius esse nec desiderabilius. . . . Finis igitur desiderii est infinitus*": "Indeed, intellectual desire is borne on not into that which is capable of being greater and more desirable, but into that which is incapable of being greater or more desirable. . . . Therefore, the end of desire is infinite."[8] And so, says Nicholas, with exemplary precision: "*Tu igitur es, deus, ipsa infinitas, quam solum in omni desiderio desidero*": "Therefore you, God, are infinity itself, which alone I desire in every desire." God shines forth in human longing, and so that longing leads us to God, casting all finite and comprehensible things aside as it does so, for in them it can find no rest; thus it is led ever onward *from* God who is the beginningless beginning *to* God who is the endless end.[9] One sees God, then, under the form of a certain rapture of the mind, and thus discovers that the intellect cannot find true satisfaction in anything that it wholly understands, any more than it could in something that it understands not at all; rather, it must always seek "*illud quod non intelligendo intelligit*": "that which it understands through not understanding."[10] And so, then, it is only within God's own infinite movement of love that any rational desire exists, coming from and going toward the infinite that gives it being.

Infinity itself, which alone I desire in every desire. And yet, for Nicholas, quite unlike Leopardi, this very insatiability—this indomitable longing for the infinite within each stirring of finite longing—is also a kind of ecstasy, an eros that finds its highest possible delight precisely in its own perpetual dissatisfaction. Where Leopardi (in his Schopenhauerian way) sees only evidence of the blind, indeterminable striving of idiot will, Nicholas recognizes from the first that nothing could actually prompt an appetite for the infinite that is truly capable of drawing us toward finite ends except a real intelligible horizon of rational longing, against which the intellect can measure and evaluate any finite object of desire. Every limited terminus of rational desire, then, is recognizable to the intellect only and precisely as a contraction and mediation of that formally limitless terminus. And so Nicholas sees this exquisite state of elated frustration as nothing less than the original intentionality of spirit toward God's revelation of himself *in* all things, an openness of spiritual creatures *to* all things, *through which* all things are reciprocally opened up to spiritual creatures. God's *"facies absoluta"*—his absolute face or aspect—is the "natural face of every nature," the "art and knowledge of everything knowable," and so the *"absoluta entitas omnis esse,"* the "absolute entity of all Being."[11] He is the face of all faces, already seen in every face or aspect of any creature, albeit in a veiled and symbolic manner;[12] he is the infinite treasure of delight glimpsed within every delight,[13] manifesting himself in all that is and by every possible means of attracting the rational will to himself.[14] Nor is the mind's ascent beyond every finite end merely a journey into the indeterminate; rather, it is a true engagement with an end at once both infinite *and* rational, because it is nothing less than God's own end, his essence, the only possible determinacy for an infinite nature.[15] We receive the world, therefore, and the world is available to our spiritual overtures, entirely on account of this prior infinite appetite for an infinite end, this desire to know the infinite in a real "infinite mode": that of incomprehensible immediacy, unknowing knowledge. We are capable of knowing anything at all only because the primordial orientation of our nature is the longing to know God *as* God, to see him as he is, rather than as some limited essence.[16] For that vision to be achieved, however, all finite concepts must be surpassed by the intellect as it ascends to a more direct apprehension. That hunger for the infinite *as* infinite, which can never come to rest in any finite nature, is also the only possible ground of the mind's capacity for finite realities as objects of rational knowledge or desire. But for our inextinguishable intentionality toward the "face of all faces," no face would ever appear to us.

II

All of this may at times strike us as more rhapsodic than precise, but it should not. What Nicholas is saying here is at once axiomatic for any coherent theology and also logically entailed in any truly rigorous phenomenology of the act of rational volition. Theologically speaking, how could God be desired as a determinate quiddity? He would be available

to thought and desire, then, only as measured against a more comprehensive realm of rational references, as merely one thing among others,
one possible instance of the desirable. But then one would not really be
desiring *God* at all. Phenomenologically speaking, Nicholas is clearly
correct that every act of finite longing, and hence of finite cognition, is
possible only so long as there is, before and in addition to the thing desired, a deferral of final desire toward a truly ultimate end. The mind
attends to any object only to the degree that it is prompted to do so by a
prior interest in Being as such. Nicholas, we should always remember,
had quite an acute and sophisticated understanding of the relation between the mind's intentional activity and its power of apprehension.
Whatever we perceive, he argues, ascends from the confusion of mere
sense-knowledge into the intellect only insofar as the intellect actively
descends through its rational faculty to inform the senses; even the
visible, as an object of rational recognition, is unattainable by the sense
of sight if the intellectual power is not directed toward receiving it—as
we realize whenever, for instance, we fail to note another person passing
us by on the road not because our eyes are averted but because our
mind's intentionality is.[17] The same is true of all our faculties of cognition, as we realize whenever, say, many persons are speaking to us simultaneously, but we understand only what one of them is saying because
he is the only one to whose words we are paying attention.[18] But Nicholas
also recognizes that, even in these simple labors of mental attentiveness,
there is already an implicit movement of the intellect beyond any immediate intuition and toward infinity. It is not, he says, our animal powers
or "spirits" (in the physical sense of the subtle virtues of the brain and
organs of the body) that recognize the things about us, but the "higher
spirit" of discrimination,[19] and the more we follow that light of reason
up to its source, ascending from mere sense-perception, the more we become conscious of our prior intellectual awareness of the infinite light
of God knowing in us and drawing all to himself.[20]

It is worth pausing here to consider the force of Nicholas's reasoning.
In one sense, really, he is merely calling attention to a plain fact of experience. It is obvious that the intellectual knowledge of any object involves
a kind of attentiveness that is prompted by a more capacious desire to
know "in general." It is equally obvious that no discrete finite end is the

original source of this desire, as finite knowledge is by its nature an act of recognition, evaluation, judgment, and choice in light of ends that precede and exceed the particular object of such knowledge. So any run-of-the-mill Neoplatonist could tell us that all rational desire—as opposed to pure brute impulse, if such a thing really exists anywhere in nature—is animated by a prior preoccupation of the mind and will with ultimate transcendental indices of identity, meaning, value, and desirability, such as the Good, the True, the Beautiful, and Being itself in its unity. And even the meanest of modern phenomenologists should be able to see that a rational intentionality isolates the intuitions that fulfill it only as set off against a horizon of much more indeterminate and inexhaustible intentionality. And any of us, when attempting to discover the ultimate source and end of our rational longing—the one terminus in which alone the entire energy of the mind and will can come to rest, replete in the Good as such or the True as such or the Beautiful as such—will find that this interminable deferral of desire can rest only in the infinite *as* its end. Where Nicholas distinguishes himself, however, is in how clearly he sees that, in unveiling the infinite as reason's final cause, we also unveil a real rational capacity within ourselves *for* the infinite. Surely, after all, there must be a fairly strict proportionality between what we can actually desire rationally and the natural scope of our intentional power. I may not be able to make myself a god, for instance, but I can desire to become a god to the precise degree that I have an intentional grasp of what a god is. And if, then, I constantly desire the infinite *as* the ground of all rational willing, then in some sense my intentionality must be adequate *to* the infinite. And, as extravagant as such a claim might sound, it entirely accords with our ordinary experience.

Certainly, Nicholas makes much better sense of how we take the world in, even in those moments when it seems unintelligible to us, than does, say, a modern phenomenologist such as Jean-Luc Marion. The latter, after all, in his eagerness to elevate phenomenal givenness beyond the reach of all intentionality (which he often seems to confine to the imaginative and conceptual powers of the psychological subject), has spent much of the last two decades describing what he calls the "saturated phenomenon": that is, the event of a phenomenon—whether ordinary or extraordinary—that overwhelms intentionality with an excess of intuition, beyond the power of the subject to constitute the phenomenon as what it is.[21] And this, supposedly, dissolves the last lingering traces of transcendental subjectivity in phenomenology in favor of an understanding of the human being as *l'adonné*—a pure "immersed" or "devoted" receptivity—forever addressed by a sovereign givenness beyond the limitations even of conceptual "objectivity." In fact, this only preserves the polarity of subject and object, and in fact fortifies the former in its unique and unassailable authority, even though it does so under the form of a logically incoherent but constant negation of the subjective pole for the sake of the "objective" pole's hyperbolic supremacy. So concerned is Marion with freeing givenness from the meager conceptual powers of the transcendental subject, as he conceives that subject, that he is willing to embrace the notion of a phenomenon exceeding every intentional capacity of the mind. This is a fabulous nonsense. Nicholas, of course, tells us that "The seeing I direct at God is not a visible seeing, but is rather a seeing of the invisible within the visible."[22] But note that this very formulation depends upon the persistence of an intentionality that *exceeds* the occasion of the visible, not one that falls short of it. If, moreover, one considers any of the experiences that Marion describes as instances of saturated phenomenality—especially certain experiences discussed also by Nicholas, such as prayer, love, the eucharist, revelation, or even looking at a painting—what one discovers is that what makes them so mysterious, in those privileged moments of acute awareness when they *are* mysterious to us, is not a surfeit of intuition over intentionality, but quite the reverse: the poverty of intuition in relation to the richness—the incalculable treasure, as Nicholas says—of intention. Somehow, the mere definable intuitions available to the senses and mind do not yet exhaust what one already knows or expects to be true of the given. And, but for that excessive intentionality, there would be no way of grasping the sheer givenness of the phenomenon at all; one would be fixed forever, and contentedly, in the precise ratio between a finite intention and the objective finitude of what it intends.

Obviously, the finite intentions of the empirical self can be thwarted or overwhelmed in experience. Frankly, though, many of Marion's descriptions of "saturated phenomena," especially of those in which one can report a surfeit of qualitative or quantitative intuition, seem scarcely distinguishable from descriptions of cognitive dissonance, such as one's first encounter with the "dynamical sublime" or one's sense of disorientation on taking a sip of wine from a glass that one had thought contained milk. Such dissonances are nothing but corrigible and temporary failures of intentionality. But even when he speaks of some extraordinary event, like divine revelation, which may surprise us or overturn our common expectations, he is still providing not an example of what he calls "counter-experience," but only an example of another kind of cognitive dissonance, one that can be received as given—if at all—only to the degree that it is recuperated into a more extensive intentionality. And when he discusses a sense of meaning or significance that exceeds the merely objectifiable and conceptually limited aspects of a given phenomenon, it seems clear that he is really only calling attention to the inadequacy of intuition as measured against the still greater extent of the intentionality that has opened it to thought. No phenomenon can give itself if there is no prior realm of rational intentionality where it can show itself. So, yes, no doubt at the level of the empirical, psychological self, with its wandering attention, the limits of intentionality can be reached before experience has been exhausted. But, at the level of what Maximus the Confessor calls the "natural will" and Augustine calls the "unquiet heart" and Nicholas calls that "which alone I desire within every desire," there is only a primordial orientation toward the infinite, one not constituted by, but instead constituting, the psychological self as a phenomenon; and within the full scope of this orientation any phenomenon can make its appearance, and any seeming contradiction can be resolved. This does not mean that that highest intelligibility can be reduced to calculative and quantitative cognition; ultimate knowledge is unitive, not conceptual; but it does mean that, as Nicholas says, the mind can never really extend itself to such a capacity that it is rendered incapable of becoming yet more capacious.[23]

In the end, what certain overwhelming experiences really bring to light is nothing but that same dynamism described above: infinite rational desire seeking its infinite rational end. Rather than speaking of the saturated phenomenon, then, it would be better to adopt Nicholas's language of the "symbolic" or "veiled" phenomenon of the "absolute face" in every face.[24] This is the one "excessive" phenomenal experience to which we are all occasionally admitted, after all, in those rare moments

when we become briefly aware of that open interval of the uncanny that
stretches out behind every finite thing—that distance that lies between
every finite thing and the ultimate horizon of its intelligibility—which is
the difference between the limited reality or fragile contingency of *what*
something is and the mysterious fortuity *that* it is. The event of any essence, we find, appears within the ever more embracing horizon of Being's
gratuity, a horizon at once intentional and ontological. And the surfeit of
intentionality over intuition in such moments turns out to be, not surprisingly, simply an immediate awareness of the infinite and irreducible
surfeit of Being over beings, the invisible difference between them. Once
again, moreover, this experience apprises us of an intentional range—a
deeper natural intentionality—within ourselves capable of that interval,
and so capable of going beyond the finite occasion of experience toward
the inexhaustible source of its event, the whole horizon of Being's infinite
fullness.

III

Another way of saying this, perhaps, is that our natural and irrepressible
desire to know the truth of anything and everything is the desire to
"see face to face" and thus to "know fully," just as we are "fully known"
(1 Corinthians 13:12), and so "to see him as he is" (1 John 3:12). It is the
longing to arrive at that place where knowing and the known perfectly
coincide, where mind and being achieve so perfect a transparency one
to the other that they constitute a single act. The rational will, therefore,
can rest content only in that infinite divine simplicity where being and
knowing are one event, perfected in the repletion of love. Which brings
us to another wholly delightful feature of Nicholas's reflections on these
matters: they leave no possible space for the kind of absolute partition
between nature and supernature that became so inextirpably rooted in
sixteenth-century Thomism and that held so much of Catholic thought
in its death grip up to the middle of the twentieth century, and that even
now is enjoying a grotesque reanimation among certain factions of traditionalist Catholicism. Not that this is the place to elaborate at length
on this sad tradition and its many logical deficiencies, or on the historical contingencies that spawned it. But one cannot help but think

that, had Nicholas's thought determined the prevailing impulse of the Catholic theology of the next several centuries, it would have produced a far more coherent, orthodox, and beautiful synthesis. Alas, what instead became the increasingly dominant position was that the only way of securing the gratuity of salvation and deification was to insist that, as the formula goes, "grace is extrinsic to the nature of the creature," and then to insist upon the most extreme interpretation of this axiom. Human nature, according to this school of thought, has no inherent ordination toward real union with God, and rational creatures are constitutively incapable even of conceiving a desire for such union if not aided by an infusion of a *lumen gloriae* that is entirely adventitious to everything proper to their creaturehood. There would be no *cor inquietum* within us were it not for a wholly superadded spiritual motive of which our bare nature could never conceive even the faintest agitation. That we do feel such a longing for the supernatural, moreover, is supposedly an entirely contingent fact of the present providential order of this world. It would be perfectly possible, says this tradition, for God to create a world in a state of "pure nature" wherein rational creatures, possessing a human nature identical to our own but not superelevated by grace, would find that their natural rational wills could rest perfectly satisfied in an entirely natural end. Such creatures would be capable of a kind of intellectual velleity toward God only insofar as he might be the best possible explanatory principle of the world; but this would be no more than an elicited curiosity about the causal history of things, not a true yearning for union with the divine. Nature as such not only has no claim on grace; in itself, it is incapable of desiring grace.

Again, the problems with this way of thinking are too numerous to treat here. What is worth dwelling upon is how beautifully Nicholas demonstrates that there is no such thing as rational desire that is not a desire for the infinity of God in himself, and so no natural impulse of a truly rational will that is not already—and even more originally—supernatural. "Pure nature" is an atrocity of reason. Even God could not create a rational will not oriented toward deifying union with himself, any more than he could create a square circle, a married bachelor, a two-dimensional cube, or a morally and intellectually competent supporter of Donald Trump. In fact, for Nicholas, the very structure of all finite rational desire is nothing other than a created participation in the infinite movement of the divine life: the Father knowing himself perfectly in his Logos, such that his being and his knowing are one and the same reality, consummated in the love of the Spirit. And the radical implication of this way of seeing things is that the immanent telos of God's own life and the transcendent telos of the life of a spiritual creature are, formally and finally, one and the same telos: the divine essence, understood as the perfect repletion of God's life of love and knowledge. As God is God in the eternal and eternally accomplished movement *of* God *to* God, so we are gods in the process of becoming God solely by virtue of always existing within that movement, proceeding from the same source and toward the same end; we do so in the mode of finitude, contingency, and successiveness, and so are not God *in se*; but teleologically we are nothing *but* God. There is no "place" other than "in him" where a spiritual creature can live and move and have its being and so seek its ultimate end— which is to say, the fullness of reality that God is. In fact, it might not be wrong to say that, for Nicholas, the difference between God and spiritual creatures is in some sense ontologically modal: it is the difference, that is, between the infinite simplicity of divine being, on the one hand, in whom there is a perfect *identity* of knower and known or of essence and existence (this latter is not Nicholas's terminology, of course) and the finite dynamism of created being, which directly participates in that divine reality but only under the form of a perpetual *synthesis* of knowing and being known.

Certainly Nicholas insists that the rational will can never rest in God as in another thing, an extrinsic end among other extrinsic ends, but must rest in him only as in the *non aliud*, the "not-other," desired precisely *as* not-other.[25] For one thing, he notes, God's seeing is also his being—his life is his loving knowledge of his own boundless fullness of being—and hence we exist only because God looks upon us and thereby grants us being: "*ideo ego sum quia tu me respicis*," "I am, therefore, because you regard me."[26] For another, the created intellect's true conception of any finite being is as an image of the fullness of the divine simplicity; and the created mind's assimilation of Being's boundless diversity is a participatory recapitulation of the divine mind's act of creating beings in knowing them.[27] And then, yet again, this positively requires the complementary formula that, just as God's seeing *of* himself is also his being seen *by* himself, so his seeing *of* all creatures is also his being seen *by* all creatures.[28] And then also, conversely, God is visible insofar as the creature exists, which is in just such degree as the creature sees God.[29] In short, there is no space in which the natural can exist, especially in spiritual creatures, apart from its prior and total constitution by and within the supernatural—by and within, that is, God himself. The very ground of our creaturehood, in its every actuality, is divinity. All natural knowing and desiring is a modality of divine knowledge and love, and nothing else. No absolute ontological caesura is possible between them. This is what makes the meditations of *De visione dei* so exhilarating: Nicholas's profound understanding of the shape of every rational nature's necessary relation to God, both insofar as God enfolds creation within himself and insofar also as he unfolds creation from himself. For a finite intellect, everything unfolded and distinct is a created exemplar of what is enfolded in God's boundless actuality and power, never achieving perfection as an image of that power (given every finite thing's mutable and composite nature), but allowing the created intellect to enfold it within its own thinking and thereby increasingly to become a mirror of the divine simplicity. By this mirroring, the intellect becomes an ever more luminous icon of the divine act of creating in knowing and of knowing in creating, and participates ever more deeply in the ultimate divine identity of thought and being. And there is no other kind of rational knowledge. All things are faces of the one face of faces, forms of the one form of forms, and so there is nothing the mind can know or love that is not already a divine disclosure, a supernatural revelation.

It would perhaps be best to leave off here, but I cannot forbear to make one additional observation. To a very great degree, Nicholas's understanding of this delicate interplay of implication and explication, enfolding and unfolding—which, so to speak, interweaves the natural and the supernatural, or the created and the divine, in the single seamless fabric of being and knowing, divine disclosure and human assimilation— is very much shaped by his Christology. For him, it is obvious, that what is revealed in Christ is anything but a paradox, much less a merely extrinsic union between essentially incommensurable natures; rather, it is the perfection of an essential unity revealed in its original and ultimate perfection. It is only in your human nature, says Nicholas to Christ, that I see what is in your divine nature. "*In te autem filio hominis filium dei video quia ita es filius hominis quod filius dei*": "Yet in you, the son of man, I see the Son of God, for so are you the son of man that you are Son of God." "*Et in natura attracta finita video naturam attrahentem infinitam*": "And in the finite nature that is drawn I see the infinite nature that is drawing." Just as that image that most perfectly mediates its exemplar is the image that "*propinquissime subsistit*," "subsists with the greatest nearness," within the truth it images forth, "*sic video naturam tuam humanam in divina natura subsistentem*," "so I see your human nature subsisting within your divine nature." Of course, one thus sees the divine nature in a human way; but then, conversely, one also sees the image joined immediately to its exemplar.[30] In Christ's human—which is to say, rational—nature, we see the rational human spirit in its most intimate and most natural unity with divine Spirit, which is absolute reason, and the most intimate and natural unity of human intellect with divine intellect.[31] And so on. One should not let the sheer grandiloquence of these apostrophes to the God-man distract one from their deepest import, or from the rigorous logic informing them. Because what Nicholas is also saying here, simply enough, is that in Christ the fullness of human nature is revealed precisely to the degree that it perfectly reveals the divine nature of which it is the image, and that human spirit achieves the highest expression of its nature only to the degree that it is perfectly united with divine Spirit. That is, in Christ we see that the only possible end for any rational nature is divine because such also is its ground; apart from God drawing us from the first into ever more perfect union with himself, we do not exist at all. We are nothing but created gods coming to be, becoming God in God, able to become divine only because, in some sense, we are divine from the very first.

THREE

That Judgment Whereby You Judge

Beauty and Discernment

ἐν ᾧ γὰρ κρίματι κρίνετε κριθήσεσθε, καὶ ἐν ᾧ μέτρῳ μετρεῖτε
μετρηθήσεται ὑμῖν.

———

[For by that judgment whereby you pass judgment you shall
be judged, and in whatever measure you measure it shall
be meted out to you.]
—Matthew 7:2

I

For the most part, modern philosophy is quite comfortable with the assumption that ethics and aesthetics are strictly distinct fields of inquiry, coming into contact with one another (if at all) only accidentally, perhaps inadvertently, and always in passing. Indeed, this is so much the case that it scarcely qualifies as a rule of method; it functions as a tacit habit of thought, a property of the conceptual and semantic atmosphere of the philosophical environment, and for precisely that reason the partition between the two fields is all but impermeable. Ethics is the language of obligation, aesthetics the language of sensibility; and what does the one have to do with the other? Except in certain ideological critiques of culture—of the sort, for instance, that arraign aesthetic hierarchies for some perceived sinister association with social and political hierarchies, or the sort in which issues of economic justice are addressed chiefly in terms of cultural consumption—the two spheres tend to pursue their own proper, distinct, stately, and wholly unrelated rotations. It was not ever thus, however, as even a casual acquaintance with ancient thought reveals. Plato's *Symposium*, for instance, is as much a moral treatise as it is a treatise on love or on the relation between sensuous and supersensuous beauty; and it is so not by analogy or by a mere juxtaposition of otherwise disparate themes, but in quite an integral way, as an indivisible unity. But the story of the modern dissociation of ethics and aesthetics—which, no doubt, could be told in countless ways—is not my topic here. How slowly or suddenly, insidiously or naturally, it occurred is an interesting question, but it is not mine at the moment. It is enough to recognize the estrangement as a *fait accompli*. One can, though, fairly easily identify the juncture in Western thought where it assumed its first explicitly systematic form: the epochal moment, so to speak, came with the arrival of the Kantian critical philosophy. This was the point at which it was established as a critical orthodoxy and a conscious intention of the Western philosophical project that we should not flit back and forth too nimbly between the aesthetic and the moral.

Certainly, it is Kant who assures us that the distinct realms of pure reason, practical reason, and judgment require each its own order of intelligible laws; and assures us also that none of them relates properly to the other two except obliquely, by way of an occasional and purely proportional analogy. The apprehension of natural teleology, for instance, may by extension help to provide us with some kind of purely intuitive index of moral purpose, at least analogically; but we should never confuse the one for the other. For Kant, aesthetic judgments can never be anything more than reflective determinations of those "subjective universals" under which the experiences of beauty and sublimity might be subsumed. The only rule for distinguishing the one from the other, moreover, is scale—or, rather, the proportion between our immediate sensory intuitions and the capacity of our cognitive powers to comprehend them. The beautiful, he believed, in its finite and finished specificity, can be wholly comprised by cognition, and so can allow for a free play between understanding and imagination, providing us a pleasure that requires neither any prior determinate concept nor any posterior judgment (except that of the "form of finality"). The sublime, by contrast, exceeds comprehension in its arithmetical or dynamical magnitude and thereby obliges us to venture concepts that exceed the sensory; in this way, the experience of the sublime surpasses our powers of representation, at once provoking reason's abstract conceptual powers and awakening the mind to its own rational liberty from the limitations of sensible nature. Here alone, then, the Kantian critical project allows a glimpse within the aesthetic of, if nothing else, a moral capacity: that possibility of noumenal freedom that announces itself within the experience of a certain kind of cognitive surfeit. But that is all. At the threshold of practical reason, aesthetic judgment reaches its limit, and can offer no guide to the content of the ethical; it can merely, at a distance, survey a promised land that it may never enter.

It could scarcely be otherwise, of course, given the austere limits set by the transcendental deduction. For Kant, any metaphysical speculation beyond a scrupulously chastened "metaphysics of morals" must be thwarted by the limits of reason's apparatus of perception. Whereas an older metaphysics had allowed for an ultimate coincidence of the transcendental perfections—truth, goodness, beauty, let us say—in the simplicity of an ontological source beyond the finite, for Kant all the adventures of the speculative intellect must end at the wall of the antinomies, still as yet unresolved with one another. He was wrong, of course, as even the next generation of German idealist philosophers so clearly grasped. And, unregenerate Neoplatonist that I am, I think it obvious that—had Kant attended not merely to the formal conditions of reason, but to rational consciousness as an irreducibly intentional act, reflexively conscious of itself—he might not have fallen prey to these dreary "cognitivist" superstitions. The formal structure of finite perception is something quite posterior to the act of reasoning; it is merely the last result and bare residue of the mind's persistent engagement with a transcendent realm beyond the limits of sensible nature—a realm where the mind already enjoys a direct and always primordial knowledge of certain eternal and transcendental verities. Moreover, that transcendent terminus toward which the intentionality of consciousness is forever turned continually discloses itself in the constant, if always incomplete, convergence of the mind's transcendental ecstasies in the life of reason: in the way, for instance, we occasionally find an act of moral goodness strangely and compellingly lovely, or in the way we experience the discovery of a particular truth to be a moral good in itself (and so on). This is, if nothing else, an evident phenomenological fact. For Kant, the differing regions of critical reason stand apart from one another, irresolubly heterogeneous, inviolably distinct. But it is the classical Christian (and pagan, Jewish, Muslim, etc.) view of the matter that in fact corresponds to our actual experience of reality: in the interweavings of our transcendental longings and intuitions here below, we have a foretaste of the ultimate revelation of their perfect coincidence in the divine nature there above.

More to the point here, I would argue that beauty possesses a unique eminence in our experience of this ultimate coincidence. The Good, the True, and the Beautiful, Being and Unity—or however one might arrange the transcendental taxonomy—constitute the transcendental horizon of consciousness in its every rational movement. But, in a sense, for finite spirits the beautiful constitutes, as it were, the transcendental horizon of the transcendentals themselves. No other among them, from the vantage of this world, is so obviously an intrinsically desirable end. This is precisely because beauty *in itself* elicits only our delight, rather than our sense of ethical obligation or epistemic submission or animal needs, and does so before and apart from any further kind of imperative—utilitarian or selfish—in a way that, say, the Good or the True does not (at least, not self-evidently). These latter can all too easily be mistaken as desirable for purely consequentialist reasons. Of the Beautiful this is not so. In a sense, beauty is the very splendor of transcendentality as such, morally pure precisely because it is never reducible to mere moral purpose, or to any purpose beyond itself. Thus, for instance, we know we have cultivated true virtues within ourselves (as opposed merely to a disinterested obedience to laws of behavior external to our own wills and desires) when we find ourselves able to delight spontaneously in the pursuit of goodness, or able to take a genuinely deep satisfaction—a genuinely intense aesthetic transport, I would even say—in the practice of charity.

What, after all, is it that fascinates or compels us in those moments when we encounter the beautiful in its most generous expressions? What calls us to itself, away from our own small and particular interests and predilections, in a canvas by Chardin, in Bach's second unaccompanied violin partita, in Rublev's icon of Abraham's angelic visitors? It is never merely some objective or concrete aspect of its composition. Nor, certainly, is it merely the neural effect it has on us, or some pleasing set of associations, or even some obvious appeal to our sentiments. Even the greatest degree of artisanal virtuosity by itself can leave us quite unaffected if there is not something in addition, something at once elusive and ubiquitous that shines through the mere craft of the work, the mere proficiency. The most polished technique can impress us, even momentarily enchant us, but it cannot truly awaken anything in us if the work itself fails to recommend and offer itself, however mysteriously, as something at once utterly inevitable in its fittingness and yet utterly needless in its existence. If this seems somewhat vague, I am sorry for that. But it seems clear to me that the special delight provided by a genuine encounter with beauty is in great part an irreducible sense of the sheer, needless event of the beautiful in every particular, unanticipated instance of its disclosure—the gratuity with which it manifests itself, or gives itself. It is an ontological fortuity to which our disinterested appreciation corresponds, and so we see it *here* as we would not elsewhere. What transforms the merely accomplished into the revelatory is this invisible nimbus of utter gratuity. Works that fall into this class command our regard not by oppressing us with what *must* be, and certainly not by their utility or banausic value as commodities, but entirely by their freely imparted and irreplaceable contingency. In a sense, the experience of beauty is our most privileged encounter with the difference between Being and beings—between, that is, the ontological source that cannot not be and the finite realities (ourselves among them) that might never have been but for an outpouring of grace. In a sense, the experience of the Beautiful always takes us back to that primal moment of sheer existential wonder that is the beginning of all speculative wisdom and all spiritual yearning. This amazement perhaps lies always just below the surface of our quotidian consciousness; but beauty stirs us from our habitual forgetfulness of the wonder of being, reminding us that the fullness of reality, which far exceeds the moment of its disclosure, graciously condescends to show itself, again and again, in the finitude of an event: of a mere instance. It is an experience that re-stores us momentarily to something like the innocence of childhood. If, that is, we have eyes to see and ears to hear.

Having said this, however, I have to add that this is only one side of our encounter with beauty. There is another, equally constant and crucial feature of any act of critical discrimination that is all too easily, and all too frequently, wholly overlooked. Every act of evaluation—this is good, this is true, this is beautiful, and so forth—is an act of rational deliberation and judgment, if only in the trivial sense of attaching a predicate to a sub-ject and then perhaps assigning that predicate a degree—this is *very* good, this is *partially* true, this is *somewhat* beautiful, and so on. But, then, how can any act of judgment not be in some sense reflexive or even reciprocal? How can one judge without passing a judgment on oneself in that very act? Or, rather, without submitting to a judgment from beyond oneself? In venturing any judgment, one does not only evaluate something—an object, an act, an idea—in light of one or another transcendental stan-dard; one exposes oneself to that same light, subjects oneself to that same standard, and thereby reveals oneself as a sound or unsound judge: either a saint or a sinner, a sage or a fool, a god or a monster, or (more typically) something somewhere in between the one or the other. That judgment whereby one judges is *always* also a judgment whereby one is judged. This is not only a spiritual admonition, a warning regarding the provi-dential calculus in the ultimate balance of all things, a reminder that the eye of God is ever upon us. It is also a truth of ordinary experience and elementary reasoning. Thus, every act of judgment is to that extent an act of "moral" discrimination, if not as regards the object of our evaluation, at least as regards what we reveal ourselves to be through our evaluation of that object.

II

Perhaps I should retreat a step of two from that claim and then approach it again from a slightly different angle. Let me juxtapose two scenes of "judgment" that, on the face of it, might appear to have little in common.

First:

τότε ἀποκριθήσονται καὶ αὐτοὶ λέγοντες· κύριε, πότε σε εἴδομεν πεινῶντα ἢ διψῶντα ἢ ξένον ἢ γυμνὸν ἢ ἀσθενῆ ἢ ἐν φυλακῇ καὶ οὐ διηκονήσαμέν σοι; τότε ἀποκριθήσεται αὐτοῖς λέγων· ἀμὴν λέγω ὑμῖν, ἐφ' ὅσον οὐκ ἐποιήσατε ἑνὶ τούτων τῶν ἐλαχίστων, οὐδὲ ἐμοὶ ἐποιήσατε. καὶ ἀπελεύσονται οὗτοι εἰς κόλασιν αἰώνιον, οἱ δὲ δίκαιοι εἰς ζωὴν αἰώνιον.

———

[Then they too will answer, saying, "Lord, when did we see you hungry or thirsty or a stranger or naked or ill or in prison, and did not attend to you?" Then he will answer them, saying, "Amen, I tell you, inasmuch as you did not do it to one of the least of these my brothers, neither did you do it to me." And these will go to the chastening of that Age, but the just to the life of that Age.]

(Matthew 25:44–46)

Then, second:

Archaïcher Torso Apollos

Wir kannten nicht sein unerhörtes Haupt,
darin die Augenäpfel reiften. Aber
sein Torso glüht noch wie ein Kandelaber,
in dem sein Schauen, nur zurückgeschraubt,

sich hält und glänzt. Sonst könnte nicht der Bug
der Brust dich blenden, und im leisen Drehen
der Lenden könnte nicht ein Lächeln gehen
zu jener Mitte, die die Zeugung trug.

Sonst stünde dieser Stein entstellt und kurz
unter der Schultern durchsichtigem Sturz
und flimmerte nicht so wie Raubtierfelle

und bräche nicht aus allen seinen Rändern
aus wie ein Stern: denn da ist keine Stelle,
die dich nicht sieht. Du mußt dein Leben ändern.

———

[We never knew his stupendous head,/ wherein the apple of the eye grew ripe. But/ still his torso glows like a candelabra,/ in which his gaze, now turned down,// still abides and gleams. Else could not the bow/ of the breast dazzle you, and in the slight twisting/ of the loin a smile could not extend/ to that midpoint that bore the power of begetting.// Else this stone would be disfigured and thwarted/ below the shoulders' transparent plunge/ and would not glisten so, like the fur of a beast of prey,// nor erupt out of all its contours/ so like a star: for there is no place there/ that does not see you. You must change your life.]

(Rainer Maria Rilke, *Neue Gedichte, anderer Teil*)

I know that I risk seeming a mite perverse in saying this, but, to my mind, both quotations are talking about much the same thing, albeit in very different registers and employing very different figural grammars. It may appear, I admit, that I am attempting here to make a very tenuous analogy indeed seem like a univocity, or even that I am attempting to conceal an equivocity behind a homonym. But I think I am doing nothing of the sort. Both of these scenes are, at the very least, scenes of judgment. But what they have in common goes beyond that. Each concerns not only the judgments we pass, but also the judgment we invite upon ourselves when we either recognize or fail to recognize an urgent truth that is directly confronting us. So I would insist that I am not using the word *judgment* equivocally here. True, in the first case we are presented with the spectacle of God's eschatological verdict upon our souls, and in the latter with a quiet portrait of a nameless man or woman absorbed in a critical appraisal of an ancient work of art. The situations seem hardly comparable. And, speaking in purely technical terms, between forensic deliberations and aesthetic evaluations there is, as a rule, very little commonality. What I want to point out, however, is that in either case the judgment described is not the work of our own critical intellects; neither conversely is it simply an extrinsic verdict upon our merits or malfeasances; rather, it is at once our arraignment before a superior power and our own awakening to a moral truth that is revealed about us by our ability or inability to understand something that has made an immediate demand upon us. Admittedly, the relative stakes in the two scenes seem vastly incommensurable with one another. In the former case, the failure to see the face of Christ in the poor and the infirm and refugees and prisoners is the soul's condemnation; in the latter, a failure of sensibility would be—though happily here it is not—a failure also to hear a summons issued to something deep in the soul's most essential nature. In the former, one risks being found damnable; in the latter, one risks being exposed as a philistine. Even so, in both instances the spiritual and the aesthetic converge and combine in a single moment of discernment, discrimination, and moral clarity; and in both cases—though this may not be perfectly obvious in either—the ultimate criterion of moral truth is beauty.

It is easier to see this to be the case, obviously, in Rilke's sonnet, and especially in that final, oracular imperative. This is certainly the poem's most mysterious phrase; and yet, somehow, it is also the most immediately comprehensible. I am fairly sure that it describes something all of us have experienced, even if only fleetingly, in moments of unanticipated grace, but that practically none of us knows how to translate into words: an almost numinous instant of awareness that suddenly seizes us when we are in the presence of a truly inspired work of artistic imagination. Certainly, I know I have felt it, and have heard others attest to it, however fragmentarily and imprecisely. But, precisely because of this essential ineffability, it is something that tends to fade fairly quickly from memory, or at least from present consciousness. So long as it lasts, however, it addresses us as both a kind of invitation and a kind of accusation. In that ephemeral instant in which we become all at once acutely conscious of the enigma in any truly prodigious work of art—its needless inevitability, so to speak, or its fortuitous necessity (again, words prove remarkably feeble here)—we are also apprised of everything trivial and unfinished and thoughtless in ourselves, everything so complacently unexceptional that it can be plausibly explained only as an expression of spiritual sloth. We are always forgetful of the mystery of being, so to speak, of the sheer wonder of the world's existence, and forgetful therefore also of the frightful dereliction of squandering the finite time set before us. We are ungrateful because we are oblivious to something that has been given to us freely; and we are culpable, then, because every gift is an obligation. And so, in the moment when beauty finds us, and its fortuity intimates to us something like the greater mystery of the fortuity of Being itself, we find ourselves under a verdict, but also under injunction. At once, we are made aware of what we are and of what we should be, as well as of the enormous distance between the two.

III

This, almost needless to say, does raise the rather delicate matter of taste, whether good or bad. Horace's admonition is correct, of course, as far as it goes: *de gustibus non est disputandum*. But, to be honest, that is a pragmatic rather than an ethical rule. The truth is that, unless one has the patience of the saintliest of saints, it is generally better not to debate these matters: in part because no one's powers of aesthetic discernment are infallible, but in far larger part because a philistine is generally incorrigible in his defect of sensibility, and it seems pointless to risk an affray with someone who prefers Norman Rockwell or Thomas Kinkade to Vermeer or Cézanne. In most cases, after all, it does not matter much. And, in a few special cases, good taste can be far more trouble than it is worth. The Judgment of Paris, even though it may have been swayed by Aphrodite's promise of the hand of Helen, was no doubt a perfectly sound one; surely, one assumes, the goddess of love surpasses all other goddesses in loveliness; but it did lead to what one can only call a needlessly and unpleasantly protracted contretemps. And maybe the elders of the Athenian assizes could not help but be dazzled into submission when Hypereides granted them a glimpse of Phryne's extraordinary beauty unveiled; but one cannot help but feel that it was something other than perfect justice that was served when he secured an acquittal for his client—and even won her immunity from all prosecution as a "priestess and prophetess of Aphrodite"—simply by entering a brief flourish of ecdysiasm into evidence. Even so, all this being granted, taste is not an unimportant thing. In any of us, it indicates how we are disposed to take reality in, how we are likely to recognize what is truly valuable or venerable and what is not, and how our desires are ordered or disordered. One's ability in any instant to recognize beauty or its privation, or to distinguish between the truly beautiful and the merely pleasant or meretricious, is as often as not an indication not simply of one's personal culture or formation, but of one's moral aptitude for the splendor of the Good. True, bad taste is often simply the consequence of bad education; but I tend to think education is ultimately of little account here, and that the Beautiful has the power to recommend itself to any soul open to its advent, and to evoke from that soul a spontaneous movement of love. Good taste is not always sophisticated; in fact, at its purest, it is remarkably innocent, guileless, even childlike. And, as often as not, extreme sophistication turns out to be nothing more than a laboriously cultivated vulgarity. But the Beautiful knows its own, and they recognize its voice.

And so it is, also, that the experience of beauty is necessarily also the experience of judgment: not the judgment we pass on whatever beautiful object we might encounter, but the judgment it passes on us. In much of the gospel of John, it has often been noted, eschatology becomes almost perfectly immanent. In its pages, Christ passes through history as a light that reveals all things for what they are; and it is our reaction to him—our ability or inability to recognize that light—that shows us ourselves. To have seen him is to have seen the Father, and so to reject him is to claim the devil as one's father instead. Our hearts are laid bare, the deepest decisions of our secret selves are brought out into the open, and we are exposed for what we are—what we have made ourselves. But it is not only John's gospel, really, that makes this clear. As I noted above, the grand eschatological allegory of Matthew 25 says something very similar. In John's gospel, one's failure to recognize Christ as the true face of the Father, the one who comes from above, is one's damnation, here and now. In Matthew's, one's failure to recognize the face of Christ—and therefore the face of God—in the abject and oppressed, the suffering and disenfranchised, is the revelation that one has chosen hell as one's home. And here, of course, is where the discriminating eye is always invited to find that deeper beauty, that divine light, where a poorer sensibility might find only an intolerable burden on one's sympathies. For instance, if impoverished and terrified refugees arrive by the thousands at our southern borders, bearing their children with them, driven from their homes in El Salvador and Guatemala and Honduras by monstrous violence and hopeless poverty, much of it the long-unfolding consequence of our own barbaric policies in Central America, and our foul, degenerate, vicious, contemptible, worthless, brutishly stupid sociopath and dropsical orange goblin of a president and the little horde of oleaginous fascists who slithered out of the spiritual sewer by his side react by imprisoning the adult asylum seekers and abducting and caging their children, subjecting all of them to the most abominable psychological torture, degradation, and despair in order to terrify other refugees who might also come seeking shelter here, we need not doubt for a moment that these monsters have thereby truly revealed themselves as damnable and, in fact, already damned. And, if a good number of our fellow citizens are aware of these atrocities and continue to lend their support to the fiends who have committed them, we can say with perfect certitude that those citizens have thereby revealed themselves to be—even if they are so deluded and blasphemous as to call themselves Christians—children of the devil, who have chosen the side of the goats rather than the sheep. Of this, Christ has given us firm and delightful assurances.

But I am beginning to digress. Let me simply say, then, that even hell exists only as the result of a defect of our sensibilities. The worst varieties of bad taste are, as we all probably know, forms of moral corruption. There is a historically elusive but currently very popular stream of Eastern Christian spiritual tradition that tells us that the fires of hell are only the glory of God that must at the last, when God brings about the final restoration of all things, pervade the whole of creation; for, although that glory will transfigure the whole cosmos, it will inevitably be experienced as torment by any soul that willfully seals itself against love of God and neighbor. To such a perverse and obstinate nature, the divine light that should enter the soul and transform it from within must seem instead like the flames of an exterior chastisement. A hardened heart, as we know even in this world, is already its own punishment; the refusal to love or be loved makes the love of others—or even just their presence—a source of suffering and a goad to wrath. And so hell is, in a sense, a consummate philistinism on the soul's part, a misconstrual of beauty as violence, of glory as terror, of love as hatred.

IV

At any rate, taste—as I was saying—can be a difficult thing. It is especially difficult within the embrace of a truly Christian aesthetics, which of necessity enjoins believers to see the Beautiful in those very regions of reality from which a conventional scale of appreciation would exclude it. The form of Christ, after all, inhabits at once a province of shadows and a realm of glorious light; he is at once nocturnally and diurnally beautiful; his is a way simultaneously of abasement and of exaltation. And these two ways are one: not two dialectically counterpoised moments within an irresoluble paradox, not a before and after, but a venturing forth from and return to the Father that is one motion, one life, one dramatic action that overcomes the fallen world's defining horizon— death—not through reconciliation with the limits it marks, but through an infinite act of *kenosis* and glorification that transgresses it, passes it by as though it were nothing. All Trinitarian theology depends upon the belief that Christ's *kenosis* is not a moment of separation, a descent from some otherworldly *pleroma* into a condition of estrangement, but a manifestation of the one eternal act by which God is God. The relation between the μορφὴ θεοῦ and the μορφὴ δούλου, if Paul is to be believed, is not one of dissemblance, but of an ever fuller revelation of the inexhaustible depths of the divine (Philippians 2:5–11). The story of the Son's incarnation, life, death, and resurrection is not the story of a divine masquerade, of a king who goes forth in self-divestment simply to return to the estate he has abandoned, like the protagonist in *The Song of the Pearl*, losing himself in the far country and then finding his true self again only in his return to his distant demesne. The Son goes forth because going forth is always already who he is as the one who reveals God, because all wealth and all poverty are already encompassed in his eternal life of receiving and pouring out, his infinitely accomplished bliss and love: he is the God he is in his very divestment and in his glory, both at once, as the same thing, inseparably. In the gospel of John, Christ's crucifixion is clearly presented as being also his glorification; it is in being lifted up upon the cross that he draws the world to himself. Even in Christ's dereliction, God's infinity is made manifest: in the agony of Gethsemane, in going into the region of death, which lies over against God in enmity towards him and his creation, Christ shows that the divine infinity surpasses all separations, the divine beauty suffuses all distances; and the resurrection shows that the Son traverses the infinite as the infinite gift, never ceasing to be the true form of God: the "excess" of his infinity remains beauty, even as it spills over and erases all boundaries. The greater the freedom of the Son's journey into this world, then, the more profound the difference spanned and the farther the distance traversed, the more surely is God God. The Father's power is manifest most profoundly in the Son's *kenosis* because that power is the infinite peace of an eternal venture of love, the divine ecstasy whose fullness is the joy of an eternal self-outpouring. Thus the divine beauty has no proper "place," belongs to no hierarchy of conventional aesthetic values. A purely idealist metaphysics of the beautiful can point in only one direction, away from the world toward the simple and transcendent source of all beauty; but Christian thought, with its Trinitarian premise, must follow the path of beauty outward into the world, even into states of utter privation, even into states of deformity that still cannot conquer the radiant form of God. Christian thought does not simply ascend to the beautiful, but finds the beautiful in the entire scope of the divine life, even as it proceeds downward into utter inanition: God ventures even into the godless, and still his beauty is there, still offered as gift, delight, and love.

This, I think, is the most radical and precious gift of Christian aesthetics: the eye of charity, which relentlessly but joyously finds beauty even where we should not expect it, and even among the despised and rejected—the vision of love that invites and compels us to find the whole glory of Being in the brokenness and humility of a crucified slave—this new depth of vision, this new apprehension of the inexhaustible scope of divine glory, this perfect unity of *kenosis* and *plerosis*, of consummate weakness and omnipotence. From a Christian perspective, the event of the beautiful is an experience, even if only momentarily, of this love that is forever poured out in all and that leads back to the inexhaustible wellspring of love. This way of seeing is finally possible only for the saint, who is the truest of true aesthetes, the truest connoisseur of eternal beauty in its infinite gratuity and inexhaustible generosity. It is an understanding of beauty, and a cultivation of vision, that transforms all of reality into icons of the transcendent, windows into the eternal. Most of us enjoy such vision only in fugitive glimpses. Our spiritual senses are neither so refined nor certainly so sensitive as they should be. We must rely on the vision of others, whether mediated to us in the arts or in the examples of saintly lives or in countless other delicate and miraculous ways. Even so, insofar as we have eyes to see and ears to hear, in the event of Christ's presence in time we have been given—and are given ever anew—the knowledge of the beautiful in its eternal truth, which is infinite love.

V

ng my topic in a somewhat elliptical and
dulgence. In part, this is because I find
o precise formulae in this area. But, in
sking a question whose answer I find
.... to wit, what is it that Christians are seeking when they
bring themselves into the presence of the beautiful, most particularly
when they come seeking beauty in the act of worship? There is, of course,
the answer that applies equally to all encounters with beautiful things:
the primordial summons that beauty issues to the soul, the call to wonder, to reverence, to an awareness of the sheer grace of Being. Certainly,
the Platonist in me—and, I assure you, he occupies a place of special
eminence, even perhaps the throne at the very center of the palace—is
quite content to leave the matter there: the encounter with sensible
beauty is an agitation of the soul, a delectable perturbation (as Plotinus
says), one that reminds it of that still higher supersensible beauty of the
divine that is the ultimate object of all rational desire and spiritual life.
Very good. But all that is true of what we experience in a garden, in a
museum, in a concert hall, in an idle hour wandering in a park. Something else, it seems to me, speaks to us when we seek the beautiful not
just as a diversion, and not even just as an experience of rapture that lifts
us momentarily out of the mundane and ordinary *now*, but as the proper
place of worship and repentance. When one immerses oneself in the
beauty of, say, a canvas by Titian, a poem by Keats, a sonata by Scarlatti,
one is no doubt seeking transport, serenity, a hint of paradise. When one
immerses oneself in, say, the beauty of the liturgy, amid a sea of shining
icons, one is still seeking all these things, but something else as well: an
encounter with judgment. Not our own critical judgment, that is, or the
verdict we might pass on some artifact offered to our appraisal, but
rather the judgment that beauty passes upon us when we expose ourselves to its deeper, divine truths. In a sense, we come seeking to find
ourselves addressed by God's beauty, by everything in it that exposes
what is lacking in us, by that in it that condemns us, because this same
encounter also makes possible the grace of forgiveness, of transformation, of resurrection. We should at least know, having come in this atti-
tude of worship, that we enter into that place not merely to see beauty,

but to be seen by it. Those icons that surround us—those "wi
heaven" that are also the real countenances of Christ and all th
looking back at us, holding us in their gaze—remind us of this w
special force: *"denn da ist keine Stelle,/ die dich nicht sieht,"* "for there
no place there/ that does not see you." Standing, then, thus exposed before the glory of heaven in those transfigured visages and penetrating
gazes, we cannot help but find ourselves at once ennobled by what we see
and convicted by what we fail to see. We know that, within the common
call of the beautiful upward into the empyrean, another call is issued,
summoning us to that deeper and more mysterious beauty that persists
even when all pleasing form has fallen away, and all that remains are the
living faces of the abject and broken, "hungry or thirsty or a stranger or
naked or ill or in prison." That very beauty confronts us every day—no
less ubiquitously and constantly than the more immediately recognizable forms of loveliness and enchantment—inviting us, imploring us to
see it, to know it, to delight in our love of it. *Du mußt dein Leben ändern.*
For it is that beauty that will be our final judge; in its light we shall at last
see him as he is, and thereby also see ourselves for what we are.

FOUR

Pia Fraus

Our Words and God's Truth

I

There are many kinds of silence. There is a silence of intolerable absence and one of overwhelming presence, a silence of unspeakable remoteness and one of ineffable intimacy, a silence of total ignorance and one of perfect knowledge; and then there are silences of which we are blithely unaware and others of which we are all too keenly conscious. And it is in all these senses, and many others besides, that we may speak about the silence of God—but only so long as we proceed cautiously. All the great religious traditions, after all, as a matter of doctrine, assert that God is *not* silent, and that he speaks to his creatures in many and various ways. His voice is audible, we are told, in the thunderous deliverances of Sinai, in the eternal Word of the person of Christ, in the eternal words of the Qur'an, in the ageless utterances of the Vedas and the dictates of the *sanatana dharma*, in the oracles of the Guru Granth Sahib, and so forth. It is audible also, so all these traditions teach, in the sting of conscience, even if only as an echo reaching us from somewhere we cannot identify. And all these traditions also agree that we hear and see God's universal self-declaration in his creation: all things are manifestations of the one who makes them, divine words that tell—by their very being, form, and splendor—of God's omnipotence and glory. In one sense, then, God's "silence" is only another name for the sheer infinity of the divine eloquence. For it would be a kind of idolatry to imagine that, amid the prodigious polyphony of creation, divine speech should as a rule be discernible as just one small, singular, finite locution among others. Everything all at once is God's voice. At times, God may speak in articulate language out of the whirlwind, and we long to hear him do so—revealing, vindicating, explaining, consoling. But, even when he does not, the whirlwind itself is already God speaking.

At the same time, it would be more idolatrous still to mistake God's address to his creatures in creation and revelation for something like an exhaustive disclosure of the truth of who he is, one that we can formulate in words of our own. There is always that greater mystery that lies beyond all speech, which we can hear—or, rather, listen for—only by learning to fall silent. The apophatic strictures on the language we use with regard to God, on which all the great traditions insist, forbid us the presumption of thinking that our ideas or utterances could ever comprehend or express the divine nature in its transcendence. They remind us that even the entirety of creation falls infinitely short of the divine plenitude of Being from which it comes. We learn to relinquish the images and symbols and simple notions upon which at first, and for a long time, we naturally rely when seeking to understand who God is, in order to reach the higher and fuller knowledge that awaits us on the far side of those images and symbols and notions. The ultimate and highest end possible for any soul—so say Maximus the Confessor, ibn Arabi, Ramanuja, and countless other contemplatives—is that "embrace" or "kiss" of union with God in love, in which words and concepts have no place at all because they have been entirely overwhelmed and vanquished by the immediacy of God's infinite beauty. And even then God still infinitely exceeds all the soul can understand.

In all these senses, God's "silence" is a kind of perfect and limitless divine harmony, one that cannot be reduced to the sort of language we are able to speak or the sort of hymns we are capable of singing.

There is, however, another kind of silence, which is not a blessing (except, perhaps, providentially), but a curse. This is the state of Godforsakenness, the sense of being abandoned by God because one has abandoned him. It is the failure to hear God speak in anything, in any register: either in the vast majesty of creation or in the secret places of the heart—or, for that matter, anywhere at all. This is the silence of despair, and it is induced by our own failure or refusal to hear, and by the universal alienation of the world we live in from God. Here we dwell outside the garden, or outside the gate of the enduring city, or on the wrong side of the veil of *maya*. It is a world in which the forces that drive history onward are not, as a rule, divine justice, mercy, and love, but rather violence, cruelty, ambition, and deceit. In such a world, it is quite often the case that we can hear God's voice only indirectly, precisely to the degree that we make our own words and actions vehicles of his Truth. As often as not, what reveals God to us are our own attempts faithfully to express, by our lives and our confessions, the holiness of the divine. In part, so every sound tradition tells us, this means that something of God's address to us becomes audible, to ourselves and others, when we observe the simple practice of always telling the truth. Simply by speaking of what is *as* it is—simply by making our words faithfully mirror what is objectively the case—we bear witness to God's command that our hearts and tongues remain pure, so that we may love and confess him without profaning his holiness. This seems obvious, and largely unproblematic.

For me, though, perhaps due to some perversity of temperament, this seemingly obvious rule is fraught with all kinds of painful ambiguities. What *precisely* does it mean *always* to tell the truth in a world that strives to resist the divine presence? Is it, in fact, clearly the case that fidelity to the truth consists in fidelity to facts, even when the facts that surround us—the facts of history, the facts of an evil situation—are in reality forms of what one might (for want of a more satisfactory term) call ontological falsehood? I am not trying to be precious or cryptic in phrasing the matter thus. In a very real sense, I am raising one of the oldest questions of moral reasoning. Is it possible that there are times that our words more faithfully reflect God's truth because they do *not* conform or correspond to what happens to be the case? And, by this, I do not mean those times when we merely speak hopefully of things that might be, but that are not yet the case; I mean also those times when, out of a love of God's truth, we might feel compelled to deceive.

II

Is prudence the enemy of virtue or its necessary condition? In a sense, I suppose, this is already a prudential question, since every moral decision in life entails both some kind of general adherence to an abstract ethical principle and some kind of particular concrete practical judgment. And even this distinction between universal principles and their prudential applications is only a relative one. We exercise moral prudence only because we believe we are morally obliged to do so—in the abstract and absolutely—since nothing apart from this obligation compels us to fit our actions to the ethical requirements of the present; yet we embrace universal ethical maxims only in light of their possible consequences, since there can be no other way of determining—in the abstract and absolutely—which actions are virtuous rather than vicious. And, at either pole of the antithesis (if that is what it is), the same insidious ethical danger threatens. Where morality is concerned, either too deontological a purism or too consequentialist a pragmatism can convert a sound moral axiom into a counsel of moral idiocy. At least, it seems correct to say that all ethical life consists in obedience to the correct maxim at the correct moment under a certain set of particular circumstances, in the knowledge that those circumstances play a substantial role in determining the character of that action. It is no doubt right to believe that one should not, as a rule, forcibly prevent a stranger from walking home; but this rule does not forbid us from physically restraining a blind and deaf woman from stepping in front of a speeding car. In that situation, we know that some other moral maxim must take precedence. Prudence without virtue is empty; virtue without prudence is blind. Again, this seems obvious.

And yet something still appears to be unsatisfactory here. On the one hand, it seems pointless to think of ethical commitments as anything other than universal principles of action, and yet it seems foolish to imagine that we can behave ethically other than by way of particular acts of commonsense deliberation. And, at least at the present moment in the history of ethical reflection, this constitutes something of a tension. Modern Western ethics in particular, at least since the time of Kant, has been haunted by the exquisite lucidity of the categorical imperative. The angels of Königsberg persistently whisper in our ears that an action cannot be truly morally good unless its implicit principle could also serve as a universal maxim of behavior in every possible situation. But, in the moment of decision, even the determination of which aspect of our actions constitutes their functional "principle" is a prudential labor of interpretation. And this seems to leave us without a rule of action any more precise than, say, *"Dilige et quod vis fac"* (to quote Augustine, that notorious relativist)—"Love, then do as you will." What is the poor ethicist to do? Nor is the dilemma exclusively a modern one. True, it was Kant who propounded a deontological ethics so severe and pure that it would prevent one from telling a lie even if one believed that telling the truth might result in the death of an innocent person at the hands of a violent criminal. In that very claim, of course, lies a contradiction, since the reasons Kant gave for the prohibition on lying—that it undermines the rational dignity of other persons and would render social life impossible if translated into a universal maxim of action—show that even the categorical imperative must ground itself in a consequentialist calculus. Kant, however, need not concern us here.

On this score, he was no more unyielding than, say, Augustine or Thomas Aquinas, and their reasoning on the matter was far more impeccably consistent. For them, simply enough, God is Truth and so—if we are to attune our minds, wills, and actions to God and to dwell in his Spirit—we must never violate the truth with our words. What we say must correspond to the objective "facts of the matter," regardless of the situation. Thus modern Augustinians and Thomists are every bit as inflexible as any Kantian could ever be on this score. They will tell you that if, say, you were living in Nazi-occupied Amsterdam in 1944, and you knew that Anne Frank, her family, and other Jewish fugitives were hiding in a concealed room behind some bookcases in the *Achterhuis* down the road, and the Nazis came to your door and asked if in fact Jewish fugitives might be found in that building, you would be absolutely obliged not to lie. Perhaps you might hold your tongue—which would, of course, be the same thing as admitting to your visitors that their suspicions are correct—but you must not in any way willingly mislead anybody. I have even heard one Thomist argue that, in such a situation, one would certainly be allowed to kill the Nazis at the door in order to save the Jewish families down the road, but one must never deceive them. Now, certainly, I would never want to dissuade anyone from killing Nazis, if that should be the only way to prevent them from doing the sorts of things Nazis do; I am no pacifist. But, for argument's sake, let us assume that this option does not exist. You are ninety years old, confined to a wheelchair, unarmed, and all alone. Indeed, while we are at it, we might as well add that you are blind and manacled to your chair. Even then, so warns the Thomist or the Augustinian—no less than the Kantian—you must never tell a lie. God (like the categorical imperative) can be served only by betraying the Jewish families hiding in the *Achterhuis* to those who would murder them.

I do not actually believe that anyone really believes this. I know, however, that a certain number of ethicists and theologians believe they believe it, and this troubles me. I am honestly convinced that, in that situation, just about no one with a conscience would tell the truth—in fact, no one would fail to lie—except out of either cowardice or malice, even if one were able to convince oneself afterward that one's motives had been purely moral. One's ability just then to "obey" the absolute prohibition on lying to others with a clear conscience would be dependent on one's skill at lying to oneself. That, however, is not my principal concern here. Rather, what interests me is the curiously questionable logic of insisting on any inviolable moral maxim of truthfulness in a world in as much (so to speak) *transcendental disarray* as ours. Only in a world where prudence is never required, because contradictions cannot arise between what we ought to desire and what the world really is, can it possibly be the case that telling the truth—in the barren and perhaps dubious sense of simply reporting whatever happens to be factually the case, careful to make sure that one's words correspond in altogether atomistic fashion to each of the discrete particular features of those facts—is a moral good in and of itself. It is strange enough that modern philosophers should so utterly dissociate ethics from epistemology, as specific spheres of inquiry, that they can discuss the ethical status of lying in total abstraction from a deeper consideration of precisely what Truth itself might be, and so can assume a virtual identity between truthfulness and factuality. It is altogether absurd to see champions of antique or mediaeval systems of moral reasoning falling prey to the same omission. I say this for metaphysical reasons; but those reasons have moral implications. I accept the premise (as any believer in transcendent Truth must) that we must never violate the truth with our words. I simply suspect that classical theists are logically bound to believe that often our words can preserve truth's inviolability only when they mislead—only, that is, when they silence history's silencing of God's voice.

III

I assume, to begin with, that practically everyone can recognize that truth-telling and lying are actions that admit of differing modalities. For instance, I assume that most ethicists—Kantian, Christian, Jewish, Muslim, religious of every variety—would grant that there is no moral requirement that one's words correspond to any actual set of facts when one is engaged in writing fiction. A novelist who at no point in his or her text gives any indication that the events in the novel did not actually take place in the physical world we all share is not guilty of a sin, surely. In a very real sense, in keeping with the conventions and necessities of the particular virtuous action in which he or she is engaged—the action, that is, of creating a work of art—he or she is in some sense telling lies, or at least not making his or her words conform to any actual state of affairs. And yet we all grant that there is another kind of truth, and perhaps at times a much higher one, appropriate to fiction. In fact, most of us would grant, I hope, that a truly great writer can often reveal more of Truth, in a higher sense, than any mere factual accounting of real events could ever do, precisely because that Truth is rarely if ever fully embodied in quotidian events. The true, in this case, is something essentially contrary to the merely factual. But surely, then, this is not merely a matter of aesthetic license, without moral meaning. How could it be? How could the writing of fiction ever be a virtuous act if we cannot concede that Truth and fact are both conceptually and ontologically distinct, and that at times our words can serve the former only by taking leave of the latter?

So, then, to quote a prominent figure from Christian scripture: What is truth? For a Christian, of course, as for a Jew, Muslim, virtuous pagan,

Hindu, Sikh, or any other adherent to the most venerable classical meta-physical claims, Truth in the fullest sense—like Goodness and Beauty—is an eternal transcendent reality, originally and ultimately convertible with Being itself, and completely coinciding with all other transcendental predicates in its divine source and end. In God, the True, Good, and Beautiful are all one and the same splendor of the real, one and the same perfect act of being. Truth, before all else, and certainly before it becomes a matter of some epistemologically measurable correspondence between words and facts, is an ontological perfection, and hence one of the names of God. And so, yes, one must remain faithful to Truth, but one must also remain faithful to all the transcendentals, all the perfections of Being in its holiness, at the same time. And this creates something of a problem. If we dwelled in paradise, in an unfallen world, in Eden, or if we had already come to the end of the tale, in the final reality of a restored creation, in the Kingdom or the Garden or the Age to Come or Vaikuntha or the Western Pure Land, beyond every shadow of sin and death, then we would never have to choose between the good and the beautiful, the beautiful and the true, the true and the good. There would be no separation of the ethical from the epistemic, the epistemic from the aesthetic, the aesthetic from the ethical, and certainly no conflict among them. There would be only one order of desire, the rational soul's longing for God, a single pure movement of the mind and heart toward the one true terminus of every rational and virtuous longing. Ethics would not exist; neither would aesthetics or epistemology. There would be only love for the irresistibly desirable.

In the world we actually inhabit, however, the simple light of Being's splendor has been refracted into separate and at times incompatible modes of the real. The divine light in its purity and immediacy lies now on the other side of the prism of created being in its fallen or deluded condition, and for the most part we know that light as, at best, a scattered iridescence. Ideally, we should live lives in which the good, true, and beautiful are as nearly reintegrated into a single style of existence as possible; but the ideal is rarely attainable. From moment to moment, we are confronted by conflicting transcendental vocations, and moral prudence consists in nothing other than choosing which among them must, in any given instant, assume the station of the dominant value. An artist in the moment of creation must for the most part obey the Beautiful above all. A reporter seeking to expose government corruption must seek the True before anything else. And an invalid in Amsterdam in 1944, visited by Nazis who are looking for Jewish families, must not allow any value but the Good to dictate his or her words and actions. Admittedly, it is never the case that any transcendental value reveals itself in absolute isolation from all others; where the Good is present, so also in some measure are the Beautiful and True; and so on for each of them. And each is more itself the more perfectly it coincides in actuality with each of the others, while each is more spectrally removed from its proper essence the more dissociated it becomes from each of the others. The more distinct these transcendental perfections become, as different modes of being—*ens qua bonum, ens qua verum, ens qua pulchrum*, and so forth—the less fully they express the splendor of Being. Even so, it is also almost always the case that we must determine which of the transcendental perfections we should assign the highest station in the hierarchy of values at any given moment in order to allow us to be as faithful as possible to all of them together in their divine reality. Sometimes we must isolate a single dimension of Being as our supreme object of concern because it is the aspect of God's reality that makes the greatest claim upon us *in that moment*. Only by a prudential ordering of ends in a hierarchy of relative priority can we, in any instant, remain faithful to all the proper ends of our nature. So there are times when, say, a dedication to the Good must in some ways inhibit a dedication to *a* truth, or at least qualify it under the form of a dissimulation, precisely so that we can serve Truth (which is also Goodness) as such. Sometimes, if we are devoted to Truth, we must deceive.

After all, if Truth is most essentially an ontological reality—a name for Being and so for God—then its nature cannot simply be a matter of a correspondence between words and facts. In a fallen reality, there are times when the facts of the matter are ontological untruths, because they are privations of the Good. And if, moreover, we define Truth as a name for Being, and we define Being as pure actuality rather than as, say, some kind of Fregean second-order proposition about what general possibilities are instantiated in which particular facts, then we must also grant that Truth is present to the degree that it is made manifest in substantial forms and specific orderings of events; it is something to be desired as a transcendental end in itself, convertible with Goodness and Beauty and so forth, which like any such end inspires an incalculable variety of practices. At least, we must never confuse ontological perfections for personal styles of behavior. It is the substance we should seek, not some maxim for our behavior that would be equally valid whether or not it can lead to that concrete and objective reality. Just as pacifism is not Peace, but merely a form of personal comportment that may equally well serve either peace or conflict (as the case may be), so reporting facts is not Truth, but merely a use of signs that may serve either truth or (ontological) falsehood. Thus, when the Nazis come for Anne Frank and her fellow Jews in hiding, we can make our words faithful either to divine Truth or to an objectively disordered state of affairs that is contrary to Truth in its essence; but we cannot make them faithful to both. As I have said, the more starkly these transcendental predicates are alienated from one another in actuality, the less any one of them is itself. All evil is a privation, after all, the distortion of a substantial good. A certain concern for the facts may arise from a devotion to Truth; but sometimes facts are the lies this world tells about the true nature of reality, and so to speak those facts is to serve the father of lies rather than God.

IV

Dilige et quod vis fac. Perhaps, after all, Augustine's maxim turns out to be the only real "categorical imperative" for someone who believes in the coincidence of Being's perfections in the simplicity of God. Ethics, conceived as a science, can quickly become a demonic nonsense. How could it not, after all, since ethics as a discrete sphere of concern exists only by virtue of our loss of paradise and our exile in the shadow-realm of human history? Ethical theory—or, better, moral theology—serves a good end only if we understand it as something we pursue in order to correct the deficiencies of our love and the injustices of fallen time. It must flow from and, in the end, yield itself up to a spiritual attentiveness to the voice of God in the moment, as it breaks through the silence of this world's seeming Godforsakenness. Perhaps all of this is obvious. But it seems worth saying anyway, as clearly as possible, even if most of us already know it as a practical truth. To dwell in mere human history in this world—to dwell exclusively in facts—is also often to dwell in untruth. And so the law of love is not merely some inflexible ethical rule we rely upon to negotiate the contingencies of that history. Rather, it is a kind of anarchic escape from all such rules into a realm of direct responsibility before reality in its transcendent plenitude. It is a devotion not to any abstract maxim, but to a living divine word that comes always as revelation, a *novum* breaking in upon our expectations and demanding a response that cannot be reduced to a mere axiom. It is the will to shatter the silence that history would impose upon the voice of God.

FIVE

Geist's Kaleidoscope

Some Questions for Cyril O'Regan

I

Sometimes a thwarted journey leads to a better destination. I confess that, when I agreed to contribute to a volume of essays on the work of Cyril O'Regan,[1] my sights were set upon a very particular expanse of terrain, which I intended to explore for rare fauna and unnamed flora with almost theatrical diligence; but then I found that two other authors had furtively preceded me, and had wantonly carried away all the choicest specimens before I had ever set out. So I have chosen to abandon that territory entirely, and all its adjacent fields, fens, and forests, and to make for higher elevations instead, simply to take in the wider lay of the land and to enjoy the view—which is, as it happens, an extremely bracing one. I have immense admiration for O'Regan, both as a scholar and as a person, and enormous sympathy for his project as a whole. I admire especially his obviously tireless commitment to the hard labor of memory, of *anamnesis*, which for Christian thought is a sacred vocation. And I feel an affinity for his work—both intellectual and temperamental—that is far more than mere polite curiosity or general approbation. I tend to think that his larger philosophical and theological vision and mine coincide to an extraordinarily great degree; and, even where we might disagree in certain of our conclusions, we certainly seem to concur as regards which issues are most important, and how they should be addressed. He is one of that very small set of scholars by whom I am always willing to be informed or persuaded without any of the sullen resentment I would normally harbor toward someone who had the temerity to tell me something interesting that I did not already know or to prompt me to think thoughts not of my own devising. It would, in fact, be very easy (if also perhaps a little self-serving) just to offer a testimonial here and then to switch off the lights on the way out of the room. But encomiasts are obliged to speak in generalities, and I have a deeper, much more particular interest in O'Regan's work. That same affinity that draws me to his thought makes it also an occasion for thinking through a number of the intellectual intuitions I believe I share with him, and so for posing a few questions aloud that have been quietly incubating in my mind for some time now—perhaps as much in regard to myself as to him, and perhaps in the hope that he can provide certain answers that still elude me.

The first of those questions is the broadest: What really happened? That is to say, I am wholly prepared to agree with O'Regan (and William Desmond) that something occurred in the course of modern Western thought that created what might be called a "false double" or violent inversion or "misremembering" or counterfeit of the Christian story, at least as it had to that point been generally understood.[2] I can agree also that this phantom simulacrum or reverse image of what is normally regarded as orthodoxy remains haunted by—but also has come to haunt our understanding of—traditional Christian thought. And, with O'Regan, I can grant that this conceptual revolution could be seen as having assumed an almost archetypal purity and compendiousness in Hegel's system. I also assume, moreover, that—speaking purely formally—this reverse image of the more traditional narrative introduces into the Christian story certain possible offenses, both metaphysical and moral, that had been largely absent before: metaphysical, that is, insofar as this newer version of the Christian story often appears to lack much of the logical and conceptual coherence of the more classical models of the transcendent and the created; moral, in that it threatens quite monstrously to import the violence of nature and history into the eternal identity of the divine, and thereby to grant that violence an eternal validity and necessity. Where, however, I demur somewhat from O'Regan's view of things is that I do not regard it as correct to think of these developments as the "return" of something called "gnosticism" (not even as a general name for a kind of narrative grammar). In fact, I think this a category error, and perhaps a kind of false memory in its own right, hiding a somewhat more troubling tale from view—though, to be fair, it is not an error of O'Regan's invention. Much of our modern understanding of those late antique systems of thought and devotion that we now (sometimes rather injudiciously, I think) collectively designate as "gnosticism" was shaped by a number of scholars (many of them German, such as Neander and Baur) who chose to read those traditions through the violet-tinted spectacles of German idealism.[3] The result, to my mind, was the invention of a historical fiction, a bizarre theological chimaera so anachronistic in its alleged tenets and tendencies as to be utterly preposterous. Nothing of the sort could ever have actually existed in the late antique world, and even before the discoveries at Nag Hammadi we had more than sufficient evidence that nothing of the sort ever had. And yet, in the secondary scholarly literature, it has enjoyed many generations of rude vitality. I will dilate on this below, however. Here I will simply say that I do not believe that there has been a "gnostic return in modernity." Or, rather, I do, in the sense that I believe that a dimension of religious discourse and thought that we might call "gnostic" is always arising anew in Christian history, but only because it has always been an integral aspect of aboriginal Christianity: a certain spiritual suspicion or agitation or disquiet, typically latent but also frequently resurgent, intrinsic to the very substance of the gospel in its first, apocalyptic proclamation. And I think that this dimension must necessarily persist so long as any trace of original Christianity remains alive within Christian tradition, and that its ultimate disappearance would be also the final eclipse of the Christian kerygma. Far from nurturing and sheltering a spectral recrudescence of the ancient gnostic systems, I would argue, the theological appropriation and use of Hegel's system (along with all its most salient precursors and sequels, whether Jakob Böhme's mystical theology or the systematic theology of many more recent Lutheran thinkers) is an attempt to accomplish exactly the opposite:

the final exorcism of a vital spiritual presence within Christian thought, typically suppressed or forgotten or dismissed as gnosticism, but perennially active and even occasionally enlivening. As for the true genealogy of modernity's "false double" of the Christian story, conversely, I think it nothing more than a grim but probably inevitable—even, I would argue, somehow natural—metastasis of certain elements unique to what we normally take to be Christian orthodoxy.

On the one hand, all of this may amount to no more than a difference between two differing historical reconstructions of a single phenomenon regarding which, in all its specific concrete details, there is otherwise more or less perfect agreement. On the other hand, however, historical memory is precisely what is probably most at issue here. Much of the special and truly absorbing brilliance of O'Regan's work lies in his recognition that, to a very large extent, the great drama of modern philosophy's struggle for the past is also a war for the future. Every age, of course, seeks to remember the immemorial, and to invent a past by which to make sense of the present, and to make it easier both to conjecture about and to determine what the future will bring. But usually this desire has expressed itself in myths or in heroic fables about times and persons only vaguely recalled. Only in modernity did it become the driving force of an ideological struggle as well. The Renaissance is perhaps the inaugural phase of this change; those of the period and (more particularly) of later generations who refused to see the philosophical and artistic achievements of the fifteenth and sixteenth centuries as having in any way naturally evolved from the culture of the high Middle Ages, and who preferred to speak instead of the rebirth of an ancient wisdom out of the darkness of mediaeval forgetfulness, were engaged at one and the same time in the invention of a classical past (based in part on reality, in part on a hermetic fantasy) and in the willful forgetting of a much more immediate past. More radical still was the later mythology of Enlightenment, and the quaint delusion it cultivated that the modern period was in the process of wholly abandoning the obscurantisms and barbarisms of an inherently defective past, and of generating an entirely new order of values for itself out of the now liberated operations of pure rationality. But Hegel's ambitions far exceeded those of earlier generations who had devoted themselves to a labor of fabulous recollection and willful oblivion; he was not content simply to take leave of a fictional past in pursuit of a fantastic future, but aspired to a complete revision of all historical memory, in order to subsume all that had come and gone, without remainder, into his majestic epic of *Geist*. It is therefore quite understandable that O'Regan has devoted so much of his work over the years to an engagement with Hegel's project. And it makes perfect sense as well that he is now every bit as much engaged with Heidegger's. The two projects are, at the last, two versions of the same imperial aspiration, the same diegetic quest to conquer all the territories of human thought and to bring them under the canopy of a single inescapable total narrative that, in essence, renders all further philosophy otiose. Hegel's version is a magnificent late Christian contrapuntal composition, played out through all the major and minor scales; Heidegger's transposes the melody into the harmonically minimalist, more purely evocative, more plaintive modal diapason of a receding and largely forgotten pagan prehistory. But both tellings of the tale—the Concept's continuous historical diremption and sublation into *Geist*, the epochal "sending" of Being in a process of disclosure-as-dissemblance—undertake the recovery of the past as a total revision of memory, reducing the whole of history to a necessary sequence of rational or fateful moments that culminates in—or that is finally "healed" by—a speculative project resolving all the contradictions of the past. In either version of the tale, moreover, traditional Christian theology is assigned a vital but in many respects obsolete role: either that of the illuminating but still inchoate mythic premonition of a wisdom yet to be realized as explicit reflective knowledge or that of one of the most crucial and catastrophic episodes in the history of metaphysics, deeply complicit in Western thought's "oblivion of Being" and its ever more explicitly nihilistic destiny. Hegel's clairvoyant recollection of the whole of history and penetration into the inner mysteries of its intrinsic logic, Heidegger's vatic intimations of the hidden figure of Being moving like a colossal, shapeless shadow behind (and occasionally peeking out from) the veils of history—in either case, theology appears in the tale as an essentially infantile discourse, capable of disclosing its truth only retrospectively, once childish things have been put away, when religion has been superseded by a philosophy come of age and doctrine can now be plundered of its hidden speculative treasures at leisure. In either case, theology's place has indeed been usurped by its own double or phantom.

So, then, my second question is: How did this really happen?

II

It was part of the peculiar genius of Hegel—the secret of his system's power not only to encompass every antinomy of reason, but also to say anything and its opposite with equal emphasis—to recognize that every structure of ideas can be approached purely as an assemblage of binary oppositions, organized into a kind of speculative mechanism made up of interlocking and oscillating inversions. And it was part of his peculiar accomplishment to translate this insight into a massive feat of philosophical engineering, a conceptual machine so immensely comprehensive and yet so finely calibrated that he never needed suffer the least anxiety that it would not continue operating in perpetuity. Where else, after all, have the worlds of Heracleitus and Parmenides existed together in such exquisite equilibrium, each not merely complementing but also repeating and implying and requiring the other? What other philosopher ever produced so replete and total a vision of reality in both its abstract and its concrete dimensions, its necessities and its contingencies, or one containing so limitless a range of potential configurations, or one so capable of accommodating even the most seemingly enormous revolutions in thought and meaning without in the least endangering its imperturbable stability? There could scarcely be a more misleading claim than Kierkegaard's canard that Hegel had erected a magnificent palace of ideas but was forced to live in a hovel outside. In fact, Hegel's palace was a triumph not only of architectonic inspiration, but of sorcery. It could magically transport all thought and experience into itself while never providing any means of egress. And there really is no escape for those trapped within its walls, even when they imagine they have slipped the sorcerer's bonds. Even the most thoroughgoing rejection of the system can be recuperated into the system again, as a negation or polarity already comprised within its logic. The whole structure consists in exquisitely orchestrated polarities, reciprocal negations, each containing its opposite as an only seemingly dormant force within itself, and as the inner secret of its own intelligibility. Again, the best metaphor is that of a machine, a dynamo in perpetual motion, generating endlessly new patterns within itself—a machine whose design, moreover, is held together and set in action by a simple spring of vertical contraction. From at least the time of Plato, premodern Western thought had presumed something like a necessary μεταξύτης or interval between the transcendent and the immanent, the absolute and the conditional, a kind of ontological and analogical median at once uniting and dividing the there above and the here below, and by its very fixity preserving them in their distinct positions in a single hierarchy of relations. But Hegel discovered that the collapse of that interval could produce something truly astonishing, and that this could be accomplished by only the slightest revision of reason's expectations. In place of that interval, he realized, one need imagine only a kind of crystal line of division running through the middle of every discrete antithesis, the horizon of a specular and speculative inversion, like the surface of one of the mirrors in a kaleidoscope; and, just as in a kaleidoscope, it requires only the smallest adjustment of the relative positions of the poles—the smallest movement of rotation from above to below—to initiate a gorgeous, fluid, thoroughly precise but also infinitely variable spectacle of countless reversals and reflections and reconfigurations.

Nor need there be anything at all regular or static about the way in which those transformations occur. The various oppositions composing the picture need not change in synchrony with one another. Some polarities might be entirely reversed while others remain more or less as they were. We see this, certainly, in the dazzling variety of ways in which Hegel's system was received by parties of every persuasion. Theological models of the trinity influenced by the system, for instance, could invert the traditional opposition between eternity and time while at the same time leaving that between spirit and matter largely unchanged; Marxists, by contrast, were willing to invert both, but not to disturb that between rational truth and vulgar opinion; for certain Hegelians of revolutionary disposition, metaphysical and social hierarchies must be overturned, but not necessarily all the moral ones; for certain Hegelians of a reactionary disposition, both must in the end be restored to their original places, even if only at the end of a long historical odyssey; and so on. The system as a whole constitutes a kind of ontological palindrome, albeit in three dimensions: it can be read from left to right or right to left, but also backwards or forwards, as well as *de haut en bas* (so to speak) or *e terris ad astra*.

Each of its interlocking binaries can oscillate one way or the other largely independently of all the rest: necessity and contingency, order and chaos, identity and difference, unity and plurality, personality and impersonality, rational autonomy and historical destiny, the universal and the particular, being and becoming, existence and nothingness, infinity and totality, mind and mechanism, classical and romantic, and so on. And the system in its entirety, depending on the angle from which it is viewed, is susceptible of every possible characterization or interpretation: disembodied abstraction or radical empiricism, mystification or disenchantment, absolute idealism or dialectical materialism, Mandarin detachment or bourgeois conformity, historical essentialism or essential historicism, a "totalizing metaphysics" or the ultimate "deconstruction of metaphysics," and so on and so on. As long as the system of binaries is preserved, the relative ascendancy of one pole or the other within any of them is a matter of no consequence. All remains integrated and luminous and rational throughout. Even whether one regards the system as a whole as either "true" or "false" somehow does not matter. To an especially skeptical eye, it might well seem the system says everything and nothing at once, and everything as nothing and nothing as everything. But therein lies its invincible genius.

Whatever one's opinion of his system, however, I think it fair to say that Hegel—maybe inadvertently—discovered a genuine law of spontaneous development in philosophy. This kaleidoscope rotates under its own momentum, that is to say, and requires no adventitious force to turn it. And what seem like great peripeties and innovations and subversions in the course of philosophical history are quite likely nothing of the sort, but only automatic expressions of that law. Most intellectual revolutions are really only natural evolutions, most violent convulsions just the predictable effects of inertia, most apostasies merely the fully ripened fruit of orthodoxies. More often than not, it is all a matter of fashion. Any system of ideas, after all, can come in time to feel like a spiritual prison rather than a home, simply because a system is necessarily shaped as much by its disjunctions as by its connections. It requires walls no less than paths, deep trenches no less than elevated causeways, and countless locked doors ranged all along its open corridors. For this very reason, no system can endure indefinitely, though practically any can enjoy periodic revival:

Even the richest and most ingenious comes at last to seem not merely trite, but also a kind of captivity of the imagination, an edifice composed of arbitrary and barren conceptual conventions, long ago evacuated of intellectual vitality. Inevitably there must come that reflective moment when the rational soul ventures out beyond the grounds, turns to survey the estate from a distance, and sees it for the first time set off against a much larger landscape. And, just as inevitably, a certain fatigue or restive curiosity prompts the mind idly to wonder what the scene would look like turned upside down, or peered at through the wrong end of a telescope, or captured in a mirror, or perhaps in a photographic negative. And thus the kaleidoscope turns. What in all likelihood follows is not, of course, a total desertion of the past, because absolute vagrancy in a boundless wilderness is a far more terrifying prospect than mere confinement in a bounded but still reasonably spacious estate. Rather, there comes a kind of *Wiederkehr des Verdrängten*, a return of the repressed, by which the hidden negation that every philosophical principle conceals within itself breaks forth, demanding to be affirmed in its own right, and then strives to assume a dominant station in the hierarchy of truths. What has been determines what is to come, as the negated becomes the posited and the principle that once prevailed becomes a repressed memory. Deleuze is sired by Plato, but resentfully denies his paternity. This, at any rate, is the one law that I think Hegel did genuinely discover: the ultimate cause of most philosophical revolutions is, simply enough, boredom.

Why, though, dwell on these things here? As I say, I am very much in agreement with O'Regan regarding the "false double" of Christianity created by theologians enamored of (even when only superficially familiar with) Hegel's system, for all the metaphysical and moral reasons mentioned above, and for many other reasons as well. Above all else, I lament the disappearance in Hegelian theologies of that vital analogical interval between the transcendent and the immanent, and the reversal of ontological reasoning this precipitates. The moment the classical understanding of the immanent Trinity's expression in the economic is supplanted by the notion that the economic Trinity actually somehow constitutes the immanent in its ultimate identity, the nature of God becomes war rather than peace, or war as much as peace, and war as the necessary foundation of peace. In the theological system thus produced, the abstract form of a high Trinitarian ontology may remain—God's paternal depth manifesting and knowing itself in the generation of the Logos and returning to itself in the rational and joyful satiety of Spirit— but the open space of grace has disappeared, and with it the innocence of God. The Hegelian divine is one whose nature is not simply expressed upon the cross, but also fashioned through the probative negation of crucifixion as such, as well as through every other form of conflict arising out of the contradictions and limitations of finitude, and therefore one in which that violence is necessarily—tragically, comically, ironically— eternalized by its sublation into *Geist*. I am in agreement with O'Regan as well that the story of *Geist* is also a ghost story, a narrative haunted by the recalcitrant specter of the older tale it has attempted to absorb into itself. Where I depart from him is in the matter of genealogy (or, perhaps I should say, pathology). Even then, I do not want to give the impression that this is a simple issue, or that O'Regan speaks of a "gnostic return" in modernity without nuance, hesitation, or considerable attention to fine details. Still, I find the language problematic. To my mind, what achieves its fullest expression in Hegelian theology's reading of the Christian story is not the return of anything properly called "gnosticism." It is, rather, as I have suggested already, the long attempt not merely to suppress, but completely to eradicate, a certain "gnostic dimension" within Christian self-understanding and imagination; and its inevitable result is both an excluded middle and an extreme—yet still predictable—formulation of Christian terms no longer restrained by any analogical reservations. Theological Hegelianism, I would argue, has proved to be one exceedingly pure specimen of what remains of a certain stream of "orthodoxy" when it has been wholly purged of "gnostic" irony. Or so, at least, it seems provocatively interesting to assert.

My third question for O'Regan, then, is: Should perhaps the very concept of a "gnostic return" in modernity be reconsidered, or at least severely qualified?

III

As a critical category for understanding early Christian history, the very term "gnosticism" has become increasingly suspect in recent years, and not without good reason. I am not yet ready myself to relinquish it altogether, but only because I take it to be a convenient designation for a pervasive intonation within early Christianity (including a great deal of the New Testament) that assumed exaggerated and often mythopoetically garish forms in the spiritual communities we traditionally call "gnostic," and that had analogous expressions in almost all the spiritual systems of its time and place, Jewish, Christian, pagan, Orphic, or what have you. It was a pervasive element of the whole imaginative and spiritual continuum in which what we now forcibly isolate in our collective memory as the one true orthodox form of early Christianity was itself firmly situated. But this real, historically identifiable "gnosticism" has been so deeply distorted in much modern scholarship that the word has become for us today almost a cipher, carelessly associated with a system of belief that would have been unthinkable before the early modern period. And it is only in this misrepresented and fanciful form that early gnostic thought—say, that of the Valentinians, the Basilideans, or the Sethians, to take the most elaborate and astonishing examples—could be mistaken for a prefiguration or hidden wellspring of such things as Böhme's theology or Hegel's system or the middle Schelling's metaphysics. In many scholars' minds, it is almost a banal truism that the gnostic systems of late antiquity were built around one or another narrative of a divine fall, a cataclysm that somehow involved even God Most High, and that these systems also asserted the emergence of evil or defect from God's own depths, which was then followed by a redemption that effected not only a restoration, but even an advance toward perfect fullness, within God himself. Supposedly, at the heart of these systems lay a tale of theogony, of God coming to himself at the far end of a refining process of tragic loss and comic rescue. This is simply false. It is a relic of a now thoroughly discredited historical narrative. And that narrative was based upon a misunderstanding of the very concept of the "divine" in late antiquity, and of its immense diversity of connotations, and upon a failure to grasp the utterly inviolable distinction that was preserved in all the late antique systems of spiritual salvation—the "gnostic" no less than any of the others—between the realm of the inaccessible Father, or "God" as specified by the definite article (ὁ θεός), or the One, or what have you, and the created or emanated "divine," or celestial, or supercelestial, or "aeonian" realm. There were definitely schools and sects that spoke of a fall within the heavenly plenum, the πλήρωμα, and many told the tale of Sophia's departure from that fullness as a result of her mad desire to know the Father in himself. But the πλήρωμα is not God, nor is it part of God in his transcendent nature, nor is the identity of God properly speaking involved either in its fall or in its redemption.[4] God is beyond both the cosmos and the heavenly orders, fallen and unfallen alike; he is the always more encompassing reality that holds all other things in itself, even the highest cosmic sphere, beyond the reach of any other reality; in him all things live and move and have their being, but he does not dwell in or among them, or take his own life or movement or being from their histories in return.

If anything, ancient "gnostic" literature emphasizes the remoteness of God from every cosmic or even heavenly process to a more extreme degree than did most later "orthodox" theologies. Perfectly typical, for example, is the description of the true God in the epistolary treatise *Eugnostos the Blessed*, which tells us that God in himself is eternally beyond all principles and powers, dominions and subordinations, and is unknown to any creatures, and that he is untouched by any movements of becoming, by deficiencies, by dependences, by limits, or by anything else conditional—so much so that he is only improperly called "the Father of the All" and were better called "the Forefather," as he is the absolute and eternal ground of all real knowledge and the origin of all else.[5] Similarly, that compendium of Valentinian metaphysics and theology *The Tripartite Tractate* tells us that God the Father is absolute unity, alone and prior to all, the Forefather who is the source and root of the Son and all the aeons, but who is in himself perfect, changeless, ungenerated, unending, and nameless; the Good as such and hence the source only of goodness, while himself remaining forever immune from every effect of evil; the One whose form and essence are beyond the reach of all other beings, and whose depths and greatness are unattainable to all but himself.[6] The Sethian doxologies found in *The Three Steles of Seth* describe God the Father—to whom the suppliant reciting the verses longs to ascend—as the unmoving and self-generated One,[7] the unseen Father who is prior even to being—is in fact *non*-being—and from whom the secondary principle (Barbelo) eternally proceeds.[8] According to Irenaeus, the Valentinian teacher Ptolemy described God in himself as prior to being, pre-primordial, ὁ βυθός, the first cause of all, ungenerated, incomprehensible, abiding throughout the infinite ages in absolute stillness and serenity.[9] Perhaps the fullest and most elaborate description of God's transcendence in "gnostic" literature is found at the beginning of the Sethian masterpiece *Apocryphon of John*: God is the pure Monad, the Father of the πλήρωμα, beyond genesis and corruption, dwelling in immaculate light, into which no eye may ever gaze, superior to mere divinity, incapable of occupying any station inferior to anything, lacking absolutely nothing; "for he is an absolute fullness that has never become defective in any way in order to be made complete, but rather is forever perfect" (the significance of that formulation should be incandescently obvious here); limitless, fathomless, measureless, eternal, ineffable, unnamable, pure, beyond every pollution, indeed beyond even perfection and beatitude and divinity; unquantifiable, uncreated, unthinkable, not an existent thing among other existent things but instead higher than all beings; not sharing in the ages, but rather beyond all times and ages; never divided, receiving nothing from beyond; himself the source of all life, blessedness, gnosis, mercy, ransom, and grace; ever at peace, the head and strength of all the aeons, gazing upon and reflecting upon and knowing his image only in his own perfect light, the luminous and pure wellspring of living water in which he dwells.[10] There really is nothing here, moreover, or anywhere else within the remains of the "gnostics," that should be seen as reminiscent or premonitory of a description of the Concept simply in its abstract plenitude logically prior to its realization as living knowledge in *Geist*; or certainly of a description of *Geist* as having been achieved by a process of divine emanation and reflection; or yet of a description of a realm of divine potentialities awaiting their emergence into, and reflective discovery through, actuality. It is an account of the one transcendent, fully actual, and eternally self-knowing God beyond all things, as affirmed in all the monotheisms—pagan, Jewish, Christian, "gnostic"—of Graeco-Roman and Hellenistic Semitic late antiquity.

There are, it is true, texts that tell of this God generating creation through the ἔννοια, the "thinking" or "intellection," that is with him in the beginning,[11] just as Christian orthodoxy has traditionally spoken of God the Father as creating through his λόγος in the beginning. There are texts also that speak of the Father knowing himself reflectively, either by seeing himself in himself, as his own mirror,[12] or in the luminous water of life that is his own eternal immaculate light,[13] just as later orthodox trinitarian theology will speak of the Father's λόγος as his own eternal self-knowing. But in none of these texts is there any hint that the Father enters into, suffers, or recovers from a divine fall or crisis "within the godhead," or that his creative or emanative self-manifestation is in any sense his discovery of his own inherent potencies. Here, I earnestly believe, O'Regan is laboring under the spell of Neander and Baur. It is simply a mischaracterization of Valentinian speculation to speak of it as inhabiting or promoting a "theogonic genre," or as telling the tale "of the becoming of the perfection of the divine," or as presenting a "paradox" in its account of the πλήρωμα's revelation of God as unrevealed.[14] A "theogonic genre" was simply an impossibility in late antiquity, even as a latent or recessive tendency. On these matters, Valentinianism is no less "orthodox" than, say, the most recent edition of the Roman Catholic Catechism. Again, we must not confuse talk of the "divine" in late antiquity for a privileged discourse regarding only the truly transcendent God, or talk of the "divine realm" of the heavenly beings above as somehow other than creaturely. In fact, in all the spiritual systems of the time, the Father (or the One, or the Monad, or ὁ βυθός, or so forth) remains untouched by his creatures, even the most divine or angelic among them, and comes into relation with lower reality only indirectly, through a lesser intermediary, or several lesser intermediaries: the Angel of Mighty Counsel, the λόγος, νοῦς, the hierarchy of pleromatic hypostases. In all these systems, as well, there is a tale to tell of a catastrophe in the heavenly or aeonian or pleromatic or "divine" places above: the fall of the rebel angels under the leadership of Semyâzâ or Samael, the fall of spirits through the aetherial spaces of the celestial spheres, the mutiny of the spiritual principalities and powers who preside over this world, the expulsion from Eden (allegorized as a pre-temporal apostasy of spirits), the rupture of the pleromatic harmony, the truancy of Sophia;[15] at the very least (in the case of Plotinian Neoplatonism), there is a kind of constant benignly tragic departure from simplicity that must be healed by a return to the noetic contemplation of the One. In every case, however, God in the proper sense remains immune to all becoming and all change, and innocent of every evil.

It seems to me best, then, to think of the "gnostic" schools of the early Christian centuries as extreme expressions—bedizened with often tediously opulent mythologies, some perhaps only allegorical, many perhaps not—of a dualistic theological register that is already present, in perhaps a slightly more muted and qualified form, in the earliest Christian documents, and that is especially conspicuous in the Pauline corpus and in the fourth gospel. As does much of the New Testament, the "gnostic" narrative tells of a cosmic dispensation under the reign of the god of this aeon (2 Corinthians 4:4) or the Archon of this cosmos (John 14:30; Ephesians 2:2) or the "Evil One" (1 John 5:19), and of spiritual beings hopelessly immured within heavenly spheres thronged by hostile archons and powers and principalities and daemons (Romans 8:3, 39; 1 Corinthians 10:20–21; 15:24; Ephesians 1:21; etc.), bound under and cursed by a law that was in fact ordained by lesser, merely angelic or archontic powers (Galatians 3:10–11, 19–20). Into this prison of spirits, this darkness that knows nothing of the true light (John 1:5), a divine savior descends from the Aeon above (John 3:31; 8:23; etc.), bringing with him a wisdom that has been hidden from before the ages (Romans 16:25–26; Galatians 1:12; Ephesians 3:3–9; Colossians 1:26), a secret wisdom unknown even to "the archons of this cosmos" (1 Corinthians 2:7–8) that has the power to liberate fallen spirits (John 8:31–32, etc.). Now those blessed persons who possess "gnosis" (1 Corinthians 8:7; 13:2) constitute something of an exceptional company, "spiritual persons" (πνευματικοί), who enjoy a knowledge of the truth denied to the merely "psychical" (ψυχικοί) among us (1 Corinthians 14:36; Galatians 6:1; Jude 19). By his triumph over the cosmic archons, moreover, this savior has opened a pathway through the planetary spheres, the encompassing heavens, the armies of the air and the potentates on high, so that now "neither death nor life nor angels nor Archons nor things present nor things imminent nor Powers nor height nor depth nor any other creature will be able to separate us from the love of God" (Romans 8:38–39). Where the so-called gnostic systems seem clearly to depart from the more general narrative morphology is in their willingness to amplify the provisional or qualified dualism implicit in this vision of things into a complete ontological schism, such that creation is conceived of as having no natural relation to God at all, even in his eternal intentions. Not only is lower reality the work of a lesser or intermediary kind of divinity; it is wholly the product of an alienation from God.

As a result, here in the land of unlikeness, below the turning spheres of the planetary heavens, all is governed by cosmic fate, εἱμαρμένη, rather than by divine providence; and, far from achieving his essence through creation, in time, by way of a fall and return, the true God is so far beyond the reach of cosmic eventuality that this world has no ontological relation to him at all, not even of the most tenuously analogical variety. In place, then, of the Platonic μεταξύτης between the transcendent and the immanent, and of the metaphysics of participation this permitted, these schools provided only a mediating mythology of absolute estrangement, a grand epic of exile and ruin followed by rescue and restoration. At least, so we are told by the extant contemporary sources, and so their own literary remains largely seem to confirm. Still, throughout the whole of that tale, in every school, God—hidden forever in his hyperouranian and inaccessible light, infinitely removed from time and nature and history—is eternally the same. It is not his story. He has no story.

We are, I should add, as likely as not today to exaggerate just how great a departure from the "orthodox" narrative all of this constituted. A long tradition of platitudinous theology tells us that the "gnostics" differed from the orthodox in their detestation of the flesh, while orthodox Christianity robustly affirmed the material world as God's good creation. But, of course, it is Paul—far more explicitly than any other early Christian writer whose works are still extant—who proclaims that "flesh and blood cannot inherit the Kingdom of God" (1 Corinthians 15:50) and who teaches that the "psychical body" composed of flesh and blood must be transformed into a body composed wholly of "spirit" in order to enter the Age to come and to bear the image of the "celestial man" (1 Corinthians 15:35–49). Of course, in general, modern Christians have so hazy an understanding of late antique conceptions of "spirit" and "soul," and are so likely to take as metaphorical language that which Paul intends to be taken with the utmost physical literality, that it is almost impossible for them to locate Paul's language in the picture of reality it reflects.[16] We are also told that the "gnostics" differed radically from the "orthodox" in teaching that salvation comes through a secret knowledge imparted to the elect rather than through sacramental incorporation into the body of Christ, and perhaps there is some truth in this; but it is a difference of degree at most. All the historical evidence tells us that the "gnostic" sects practiced saving mysteries—including baptisms, anointings, eucharists, even "extreme unctions"[17]—while Christians of every persuasion believed that they had received a saving "gnosis." The gospel of John, in particular, testifies to "orthodox" communities who guarded their saving mysteries so jealously that they could be discussed openly only as cryptadia, veiled in allegories. Even Irenaeus did not arraign the "gnostic" schools for allegedly privileging knowledge over sacramental grace, or for trusting in saving knowledge in the abstract. He condemned them for promoting a "gnosis falsely so-called" in place of the "true gnosis" delivered to the apostles, and for inventing lavish and absurd myths. By the same token, the sins we might wish to attribute to Hegelianism from an orthodox perspective could not be more different in kind from those that can be legitimately laid at the feet of the ancient "gnostics." One may be dismayed that Hegelian theology turns the story of God's *kenosis* in Christ into the speculative tale of a divine reality both spilled out into the tragedy of history and perfected in itself through the fruitful negation of all merely historical particularity; but this is not a "gnostic" subversion of the orthodox narrative. And, if one can fairly say that for Hegel the cross of Christ in its historical concreteness constitutes primarily a moment of dialectical disclosure, one that yields explicit and properly reflective knowledge of eternal truth only insofar as it is taken as a symbol, negated in its particularity, evacuated of its historical accidents, and recuperated into speculative wisdom—though one has to make even this claim with a certain prudent hesitancy, given the system's extraordinary capacity for unresolved amphibologies—this is also to say precisely the opposite of what ancient Christian "gnosticism" asserted. To a Valentinian of old, for instance, what the cross of Christ reveals may indeed be an eternal truth about the divine (and, of course, no orthodox Christian could demur from that), but the cross was also an entirely apocalyptic moment of disclosure, one that did not reveal anything at all about the rationality of history or the truth of the universal, but that instead disrupted the order of this aeon entirely, and exposed it as absolute falsehood, illusion, and captivity. And the one historical Christ was, for these same Valentinians, the sole and indispensable savior from this world in his very particularity, the only possible mediator between this world and the Father, the one being who was alone able by his divine power to penetrate the defenses of the heavenly powers, to enter their cosmos, to end their reign over spiritual beings, and to set the captives free; he was not a mere symbol of anything.[18] How could he, after all, symbolize a universal truth, potentially available apart from his person, if the very world into which he descends is of its nature wholly alien to the truth he announces and the Kingdom from which he comes? This event of revelation in Christ, moreover, did not contribute to God's self-awakening, or help to transform the implicit truth of the eternal Concept into the explicit living knowledge of *Geist*, but instead apprised the elect of the truth that this world has nothing whatsoever to do with the true God, and is no part of who he is or of who they are. It may be true, admittedly, that the gnostic systems and the high German idealisms share, at least, a tendency to conflate the creation of the world with the fall of the spiritual realm. But even this is a very insubstantial similarity at best. For the gnostics of old, the fall was truly a fall, and nothing more. It was not understood as making any kind of positive contribution to the divine reality above or as bearing any "spiritual" fruit in eternity. It was a tragic contingency, one in need only of correction, and ultimately meaningless in itself. Frankly, it is precisely this gnostic moment or dimension of sullen suspicion and restless rebellion—this essentially dualistic intuition of the absolute vacuity of this world, of its inimical malice, its falsehood, and its final irredeemability—that is entirely absent from any Hegelian construal of the Christian narrative. Conversely, those aspects of the Hegelian system that are most necessarily constitutive of its approach to the Christian narrative are precisely the ones most conspicuously absent from the ancient "gnostic" systems: a providential understanding of cosmic history, an ontological continuity between the divine and the created, and (perhaps above all) a certain metaphysics of the will.

Seen from one angle, the most problematic characteristic of the Hegelian system is its unrelieved providential optimism. An absolute dualism, of course, is a very grim thing indeed; but a narrative monism unqualified by any hint of true gnostic detachment, irony, sedition, or doubt—by any proper sense, that is, that the fashion of this world is horribly out of joint, that we are prisoners of delusion, that not every evil can be accounted for as part of divine necessity—turns out to be at least as monstrous. It leads to a theology so deliriously insensible to its own moral ambiguities that it can view nothing as pure privation, pure absence, ultimate evil. In some sense, it must affirm that even war is good, that the *Weltgeist* strides across the stage of history when the battle of Jena (or any other battle) is fought, that God comes to himself in the death of a child no less than in a gesture of love. It seems to me that in the theological appropriation of Hegel's thought a certain Protestant enthusiasm reaches a febrile pitch, a rapt delight in divine sovereignty so total that it sees even the devil as only one of God's innumerable masks. At a deeper level, however, an eminently reasonable and providential vision within the Hegelian system may be sustained by the latent and paradoxical presence of something prior to and indomitable by all reason, a spontaneous power of becoming in some sense more original than the Concept itself. Here, definitely, the Schelling of the middle period may have been a more candid logician than many Hegelians. Hegel, quite *contre cœur* no doubt, was perhaps obliged by his understanding of the great epic of *Geist* to presume, however obscurely, the reality of a kind of "striving" or purely voluntative impulse in the absolute even more primordial than rationality or identity, a kind of intentionality prior to its own rationale, because the final cause of *Geist* can reside nowhere but in *Geist* itself, as an end already achieved. Of course, much here depends on just how Aristotelian a logic of finality may or may not be presumed in Hegel's own understanding of the relation between the eternal Concept and the diremptions of history. In the system, however, with its apparent collapse of the analogical interval between eternity and time, it is arguable that that finality is not available outside the drama of history and of the serial recuperation of finitude into reflective wisdom. This tacit metaphysical voluntarism, whether latent in Hegel's own thought or merely presumed in the thought of his theological followers—this quiet but persistent premise, that is, of some kind of original, as yet irrational spontaneity in the divine—certainly has no prefigurations in any of the ancient gnosticisms.[19] It can, of course, quite plausibly be traced back to Jakob Böhme. But Böhme was not any kind of "gnostic," at least not if the word has any cogent meaning at all; he was a Lutheran. And, of course, Luther was no "gnostic" either; he was a late mediaeval Augustinian.

Really, there is something oddly exhilarating about this particular rotation of the kaleidoscope, something sublime about the way in which the sheer brute historical momentum of a large but unstable idea can carry it onward through every possible transmutation until it arrives very nearly at its own opposite. There is, clandestinely implicit in post-Hegelian theology, something like a pure self-positing divine will or divine *Urentscheidung*, something on the order of Böhme's dark divine *Ungrund* or Schelling's realm of pure potency—the whole of the system seems at times to presume and depend upon it—but this, however bizarre a deformation it may appear to us, is merely the product of a predictable process of unbroken development within the larger Christian doctrinal and theological tradition. It is the exaggeration and specular inversion of a divine voluntarism first fully enunciated in the late Middle Ages; and this voluntarism was itself the extreme expression—and millennial hypertrophy—of a story of divine freedom that entered the Christian narrative as early as the late Augustine's increasingly bleak and pitilessly morbid theology of predestination *ante praevisa merita*. The moment in which God was conceived as acting toward creatures in a way for which theology could adduce no real rationale other than the absolute and mysterious sovereignty of its exercise, the first ectoplasmic wisp of the specter of an essential arbitrariness within God was summoned up in the Christian imagination. It was inevitable that this would produce, in the fullness of time, a voluntarist understanding of rational freedom in the abstract as a kind of pure spontaneity of intention, expressed most perfectly precisely when expressed most arbitrarily. Taken to an extreme within theology, it produced a model of divine freedom in which the rationality of God's power lay simply in its utter liberty from any rational measure other than sovereignty as such. And, taken to a similar extreme as a metaphysics of *all* rational freedom, divine or creaturely, it produced a picture of the will as essentially a spontaneous and indeterminate impulse toward a purely elective end, an end that is "rational" solely because it somehow miraculously fulfills that more deeply "irrational" movement of volition. Hegel's *Geist* (not just its theological offspring) was perhaps born from this all but inevitable voluntarist turn in Western Christian thought, no less than was the undeniably evil God of Calvinism and Baroque Thomism. That said, seen from another vantage, the system is an attempt to correct and rationalize this element of the irrational in the story; in the Western and specifically Protestant form of Christianity from which Hegel's thought emerges, there is an unresolved rupture between reason and will—rationality and intentionality—in the divine, and in some sense it is precisely this rupture that the system is intended to heal and mediate again into a rational and living unity. Seen from yet another vantage, however, the system, still being an inversion of an inversion, cannot help but retain something of the shape and color of the picture it attempts to supplant. And, again, all of these binary oppositions must eventually, as the kaleidoscope turns, shift from one pole to the other. The infinite God of absolute volition is inverted into infinite indeterminate volition becoming God. God willfully positing a history of predilective predestination as an act of omnipotent sovereignty is inverted into God sovereignly determining and "electing" himself in and through history. The Trinitarian God choosing to save and to damn as an act of perfect libertarian freedom is inverted into a unitary divine source of being electing to become Trinity in and through the drama of salvation and damnation. When the Hegelian system itself arrives amid the flux of possibilities, therefore, and attempts to impose a rational structure upon it, and to identify a kind of final causality within it—that of *Geist*—it can perhaps still something of the tumult, and even briefly contain the chaos within the appearance of a serene rational order. But, in doing this, it cannot entirely free itself from the conceptual forms it seeks to bring under its mastery. Whatever the case, though, none of this history of speculative developments is "gnostic." All of it is a particular trajectory within orthodox tradition succumbing to its own volatility.

And so, truth be told, to employ the word *gnosticism* here, even if only to indicate a certain set of morphological resemblances between, say, Böhme's thought and that of Valentinus (for instance, a taste for mythopoeic exorbitances), has the unintended effect of conflating conceptual languages that are in fact opposites in their intentions and meanings. Here, perhaps, is where O'Regan and I diverge most sharply in our genealogy (or maybe I should say our "phantasmatology") of this particular "false double." While, for him, Böhme constitutes "a highly plausible candidate for designating the alpha point of the genealogy of Gnostic return in modernity,"[20] to me, something very much like the opposite is the case: Böhme may represent a particular moment of inflection at a certain point within modern Christian thought, and even the "alpha point" of a new departure from "orthodoxy," but only because he represents one inevitable omega point in the development of a particular voluntarist strain *within* Western orthodox reflection: that exquisitely exact instant when a theological principle of remarkable consequence suddenly switched polarity, and allowed a hitherto negated possibility in Christian meta-physics to assume the status of a positive principle. But this was achieved precisely through the suppression of the last trace of a certain "gnostic" suspicion—of a certain unyielding refusal to grant the history of this world a determinative or probative ultimacy, or to see it as in any sense a true manifestation of the divine nature. Many of Hegel's intellectual heirs were, of course, all too happy to associate his philosophical "discoveries" with aberrant or heterodox or hermetic thinkers and sects of the Christian past, in the hope thereby of borrowing something of their rebellious glamor. But, in fact (and this is something of a surprising twist in the plot), this is itself part of the very project of "misremembering" that O'Regan has striven so sedulously to expose, but that here perhaps has caught even him in its trammels: the creation of a false Christian past, the myth of a suppressed speculative counter-history or shadow-tradition within Christian thought, a forgotten and allegedly deeper or truer ver-sion of the story that has now supposedly been rediscovered, revived, and properly curated only in German idealist thought. In this way, a very par-ticular and wholly modern "false double" of the gospel endued itself with a phantom pedigree, one of seemingly profound and majestically myste-rious antiquity. "Hegelians," certainly, may once have been delighted to invoke, say, Valentinus as a kind of exotic ornamental motif in the master's great recovery of the "true" Christian rationality. But, frankly, Valentinus is as out of place in the system as a Chinese dragon in a cuckoo clock.

Which brings me to my fourth question: Is perhaps the story of a "gnostic return in modernity" itself potentially an example of the very same "misremembering" that O'Regan elsewhere identifies with great precision, a false history that might too readily exculpate certain Chris-tian orthodoxies of the part they played in the genesis of modernity, and that thereby might sometimes hide the true genealogy behind a spectral double?

IV

Not that I am entirely certain that I know of any wholly satisfying defi-nition of "orthodoxy" in the first place. Like O'Regan, I want to distinguish to whatever degree I can between the genuine Christian story (which I certainly believe can be told, if not necessarily *in unica voce*) and all of its many phantom inversions or caricatures or *Doppelgänger*. At the most mundane level, of course, this requires only meager powers of discernment; cultural "Christianity" at any given moment and in any given place produces countless warped parodies of the gospel. But the lines of demarcation become ever more sinuously involved, confusingly elliptical, and gallingly illegible the more intently one undertakes the serious hermeneutical and historical labor of separating an original "orthodoxy" out from the impossible historical welter of all its simulacra and counterfeits and ghosts. And those demarcations prove especially vague and fluid whenever one attempts, from the perspective of the present, to isolate which strains of Christian thought today fall within the boundaries of orthodox (or *reasonably* orthodox) belief and which do not. For the most part, we identify the former as those traditions (be they ever so diverse in detail or ecclesial affiliation) that incorporate certain cardinal principles of a larger theological or doctrinal grammar—say, certain aspects of Nicene and Chalcedonian dogma, a generally consistent notion of grace or sin or redemption, and so on—and the latter as those that, at some crucial doctrinal boundary, seem to us to go over the line. The one set includes all those denominations or schools with which ecumenical or intra-theological dialogue is possible; the other includes only forms of heresy in need of radical correction. But then, of course, all such distinctions, if they are indeed anything more than the parochial prejudices dominant at a particular place and time, presume both the veridicality of Christian memory and the possibility of a fully persuasive historical reconstruction of Christian belief from its origins. But neither memory nor historical reconstruction proves particularly convincing here. We can speak with dangerous confidence about the "true" Christian story, as distinct from all the "false" versions; but surely one of the lessons of theological history is that the "original" form of tradition is, as often as not, a final formal construct arrived at by a process of dialectical attrition and synthetic composition, one that simultaneously sums up and invents its own past, and that thereby retrospectively reduces all other variants of the tradition, no matter how ancient, to the status of perverse deviations. Thus, for the Hindu fundamentalist of today, the one true "divine" text of the *Ramayana* is the final high Sanskrit redaction produced for the Gupta court, whereas all the local, heteroclite, dialect versions of the epic or of the stories from which it arose, scattered so prodigally throughout the various linguistic clades of the subcontinent and Indochina, are heretical corruptions. Theological history also teaches us, moreover, that the seemingly intrinsic unity of a dogmatic continuum is often much more credible when viewed from the present, as a *fait accompli*, since each of its various historical transitions seems to have been logically entailed in what preceded it. Viewed from the past forward, however, the sequence tends to look somewhat more fortuitous and spasmodic, and the final results perhaps more logically remote from their putative first causes, than certain other possible paths of development foreclosed by dogmatic tradition might have been.

I am not, incidentally, denying the reality of divine inspiration in the development of doctrine (though I would definitely deny that the distinction between the truly inspired and the perversely deviant is anything more than a judgment of faith that can never be fully verified historically or critically). I do not even presume that the past cannot really be determined "backwards," so to speak, in those magical moments in which a whole diverse ensemble of prior historical forces inexorably arrive at their true final cause, only to find that the full form of that endpoint had until then remained largely unanticipated. (One should not, after all, assume that historical time functions by a kind of mechanical causality.) Still, one has to wonder about how we have reached our present state. Much of what we today, at the end of two millennia of Christian thought, would consider more or less orthodox incorporates a huge number of elements—say, certain understandings of grace and nature, nature and supernature, flesh and spirit, the angelic and the demonic, redemption and justification, and so forth—that are not only different from, but also utterly irreconcilable with, what Paul believed had happened in Christ. At the same time, almost the entirety of the cosmology and the soteriology presumed by Paul as essential to understanding what Christ had accomplished—including a very particular theology of the hostile celestial powers, and of the shape of the cosmos, and of its relation to God's empyrean, and of the difference between psychical and spiritual life, and of any number of other beliefs—is all but entirely absent from or is violently distorted in much of the most authoritative theological language of later centuries. So all the best historical and biblical scholarship tells us. Frankly, it would be of only very dubious historical validity to suggest that, say, Valentinus's understanding of salvation was more remote from Paul's, in either shape or substance, than was Calvin's idiotic theology of substitutionary atonement. In fact, it would be plainly false. And it would be of still more dubious theological validity to claim that Hegel's system is any more alien to the theology of the New Testament and of early Christian metaphysics than is Baroque Thomism. In fact, in many respects precisely the opposite is surely the case. Really, compared to the teachings by which the early "gnostic" or proto-gnostic sects allegedly departed from the beliefs of the apostolic age, much of that same Thomist tradition is far more extravagantly heterodox. Certainly, at least, the apparently somewhat puerile dualism of certain early gnostic sects is no more repugnant to the Pauline vision of things than is the far more horrifying voluntative monism of much early modern Western theology, Catholic and Protestant alike. And only indifference to the religious and speculative language of the first century would permit anyone to imagine that Thomas or Luther or Calvin clearly practiced a faith any more consistent with Paul's beliefs than did, say, Marcion of Sinope. As far as simple historical plausibility is concerned, moreover, how do we really convince ourselves that the Jesus "remembered" by Hegel is any less fantastic—any less spectral—than the Christ memorialized in the developed doctrine of the late patristic period? It may well be that, somewhere amid the vast, roiling, dazzling flood and farrago of rival versions of the true Christian story, the one true original can be found and precisely delineated from all the simulacra and failed drafts and haunting echoes. But, when one goes in search of it as an object of either historical or genealogical judgment, one enters an endless hall of mirrors, full of inverted figures, or inverted inversions of figures, and on and on indefinitely, merging and separating and recombining—doubles doubled and redoubled, ghosts and ghosts of ghosts, endless divergences and convergences and reversals. If we are certain that the original really exists, it is only because we are convinced that the entire spectacle must have been produced by something real, particular, and complete in itself, something that would be left standing even after all the mirrors had been shattered, intact and distinctly visible among the shards of broken glass. But perhaps we are instead really only gazing into a kaleidoscope, and the appearance of a single coherent and symmetrical pattern is merely an illusion, a product of the intersection of multiple reflections of what in reality is only a random, fragmentary, and constantly shifting collection of brightly hued and disconnected pieces. Inevitably, refuge from such doubts can be sought only in the presumed authority of received tradition.

It may be, however, that the very concept of theological tradition is incorrigibly equivocal. On the one hand, it is a notion that necessarily presumes the stable continuity of certain beliefs and practices that must be in some sense unalterable, preserved by the community they define, and certifying their own authority by that very changelessness. On the other, however, it must also be a name for the dynamic continuity of a living process of development, one that preserves the truth it proclaims precisely by allowing it to unfold into an incalculable variety of unpredictable new expressions. And both senses of the term are equally indispensable. Every living tradition derives its authority from some initiating moment of awakening or discovery that can never be forgotten or altered; and yet, no less essentially, that initial moment is validated only in and by the richness, capaciousness, and perdurability of the historical developments to which it continually gives rise. Thus the concept of tradition, if it is to have any function at all, must be invoked as a justification both for what has never changed and for everything that has—every cultural, social, religious, and intellectual reconfiguration serially assumed and serially abandoned over the course of generations. This means, though, that it can serve as a justification for anything, a mystifying euphemism for whatever haphazardly happens to happen, or for that matter happens to fail to happen. Being simultaneously a principle both of immutability and of ceaseless transformation, it boasts an almost limitless plasticity. And this means also that its invocation is always attended by two equally disturbing possibilities: *either* there is no ultimate distinction between what is essential and what accidental in any given tradition (which would mean that the tradition has no inner rationale to speak of) *or* the difference between essence and accident is so easy to identify that most of the tradition's historical forms are nothing but convenient vehicles of cultural transmission that can be dispensed with altogether by true savants and *cognoscenti*. And historical scholarship is of only very limited value in deciding whether or not there really is a *Ding an sich* there, or how to isolate it from its ever-shifting epiphenomenal shapes. History provides us with the *event* of a tradition, in all its contingency and morphological variety, but not its essence; it records processes of both accumulation and attrition, of both retention and forgetting, but in so doing raises the portentous possibility that there is no discernible reason why some aspects of a tradition prove ephemeral and others perennial. Here, it would seem, only faith in the Holy Spirit and a certain patience with mystery can rescue the scrupulous Christian scholar from doubt. He or she absolutely must trust that the continuity of theological tradition is in some sense nourished by something that is never really visible—except perhaps indirectly, in the fluent succession of its historical accidents—to the eyes of disinterested scholarship: something by its very nature hidden behind the very cultural and intellectual forms to which it gives rise. Only the supposition of this truth silently abiding below the surface provides any explanation of both the tradition's persistence and its dynamism. Otherwise every historical transition could be interpreted only as a defeat. How one knows this truth, though, assuming one really can know it, lies outside most of the critical categories by which we try to judge the relative validity of this or that particular dogmatic or theological development—in something like "tacit knowledge," or an "illative sense," or the light of the spiritual senses. Unlike historical science, this sort of knowledge must involve some kind of understanding not only of the first "cause of motion" at a tradition's inception, but also of the final cause to which that motion corresponds, the "eschatological" consummation that is the tradition's whole rational meaning (ideally, in the case of Christian thought, this means a proleptic awareness of the divinization of creatures who are by nature meant to become gods in God). One can know this truth, then, not as any single discrete phenomenon appearing within religious experience, but rather only as the whole intentional horizon of belief, a sort of constant transcendental orientation of faith or reason that allows any religious phenomenon to appear in the first place, as both an intelligible form of and an insufficient symbol for a fullness ultimately lying beyond any historical expression.

Even formally defined dogmas are of only so much help here. Throughout Christian history, the formulations produced by doctrinal decisions have necessarily been of the most severely minimalist kind; and (as any good Hegelian knows) no thesis can be stated in such a way that its terms preclude radical—even radically contradictory—differences of interpretation. How many Lutheran systematic theologians of the twentieth century, for instance, found it possible to propose the most audacious revisions of Trinitarian theology and Christology without for a moment wavering in their fidelity to the canonical language of Nicene and Chalcedonian orthodoxy? In truth, the very concept of doctrinal *definition* is an obscure one. Every dogmatic pronouncement of the church or churches over the centuries has been at once the concrescence of a great number of prior theological or devotional forces and also the inauguration of an entirely new sequence of evolutions, discords, speculative elaborations, and reformulations. A dogmatic definition forecloses the further unfolding of certain currents of the theological past precisely by opening entirely new streams of ungovernable future development. Nor does history provide us with quite the tidy and comforting narrative of doctrinal history that we might desire: a story, that is, of a single dominant *consensus fidelium*, implicit in Christian confession from the first moment of the faith, smoothly and continuously crystallizing into ever more lucid and precise confessional propositions, all the while exposing opposing views as perverse novelties and heretical subversions. If anything, it tells us practically the reverse story: that of an often fitful invention of willfully ambiguous and hitherto unprecedented models of confession, usually as compromises between genuinely contradictory positions, successfully capturing something of the force of what preceded them, but only in the shape of synthetic formulations that also deeply altered much of the meaning of past beliefs and practices. In every instance, moreover, these innovations were obliged to claim the authority of the past solely for themselves, and therefore to rewrite the history they aspired to sum up in themselves. Dogmas arise out of rare moments of acute tension in the tradition's understanding of itself; and they can resolve the impasses these tensions create only insofar as a certain degree of calculating historical forgetfulness is cultivated around them, refashioning the past, purging it of the very complexities that made the new doctrinal formulation necessary in the first place. For a dogmatic definition to succeed, it is not enough that it supply us with an adequate answer; it must cause us to forget the original question. What we come to regard as "orthodoxy" and "heresy" are retrospective and (to be honest) transparently ideological constructions, and it is only natural that they should be. But, apart from faith in the ineffably cunning operations of the Holy Spirit, a Christian historian might be tempted to see nothing in the chronicle of official doctrine other than a continuous process of political crisis and historical revisionism. Nor can one simply repose one's confidence in the ecclesial continuity of Christian confession to dispel uncertainty here. Not that this is by any means an irrelevant thing; but, again, what truly persists in ecclesial evolution is something clearly visible, if at all, chiefly to the eyes of faith. Disinterested historical scholarship is more likely than not to see only the purely formal contiguity of various institutional forms over the centuries—structures of authority and privilege, words, repeated practices, and so forth—creating a façade that seems relatively stable, but behind which is hidden a ceaseless succession of immense conceptual, social, and ethical convulsions.

One can confirm this, in fact, by looking at the first and most consequential doctrinal definition of Christian tradition, that of the first Nicene Council. The Arian controversy was that crucial moment when a now politically enfranchised church for the first time officially *legislated* the proper content of the faith, and thereby demoted all incompatible forms of confession, however well established or devout, to the status of damnable expressions of infidelity. As a historical judgment, of course, this was pure fiction. Arius was in many respects a profoundly conservative theologian; certainly, in the context of Alexandrian theology, he was a more faithful representative of many of the most venerable schools of Trinitarian thought than were the champions of the Nicene settlement. He may have been a somewhat unimaginative thinker, admittedly, but he was seeking to preserve, in what he took to be a logically cogent form, the "subordinationist" metaphysics that in his part of the Christian world had served for generations to describe the relation of heaven and earth in a single hierarchy of powers while preserving a sense of the absolute inaccessibility of God Most High. That the Father was absolutely hidden from the eyes of all other beings, and that he was known to creatures only through the subalternate and necessarily limited agency of his Logos, and that the Logos was by nature inferior to the Father, was nothing more to his mind than ancient apostolic orthodoxy. Even in insisting that the divine Son was a creature, he was not adopting an especially outlandish position. Many Christians had long believed that the Logos was merely the most exalted figure in the divine court, the Great Angel or Angel of Mighty Counsel, the heavenly high priest who served as the sole "priestly" mediator between the unseen Father and all other creatures. It was simply an unfortunate reality for Arius that he happened to live at a moment when too great a diversity of beliefs had become an intolerable reality for the institutional church. In the age of Constantine, doctrinal disagreement was a scandal not so much of theology as of imperial policy. And, as it happened, the Nicene party did have the better arguments. At least, their picture of things made sense of a larger range of shared Christian beliefs and spiritual expectations, and arguably provided a richer theology of the intimacy between God and his creatures in Christ. And theirs, it turned out over time, was the more coherent metaphysics. Still, the Arians and Semi-Arians were theological conservatives, not wild innovators; the Nicene party, by contrast, was advancing a conceptual and doctrinal vocabulary with only very contestable antecedents.[21] And such has always been the pattern (or something like it) of doctrinal development.

Again, I am not attempting to relativize away all Christian claims into a kind of inadjudicable equivalence. I, for instance, cordially loathe much of "Hegelian" theology's construal of the Christian story. This is not to say anything about Hegel's own thought or about its indisputable brilliance, obviously; it is impossible not to be awestruck by a philosopher of such colossally creative originality. I nevertheless believe that what it inspired in many Christian theologians, and what they naturally spun out of it (as far as they were able), proved to be morally abrasive, metaphysically vulgar, logically incoherent, and tediously fantastic. I believe that one can demonstrate in any number of ways—logically, morally, metaphysically, aesthetically, hermeneutically, historically, practically—that there are far better and more plausible and more persuasive and more spiritually liberating readings of the record. But I do not believe that this is something that can be argued in either a catechetical or a purely genealogical mode. I think that, to the degree any one of us possesses a clearer knowledge than any other not simply of the historical and textual facts of the Christian tradition, but also of the proper reading and interpretation of those facts, it is a knowledge inspired by a largely inexpressible and necessarily imprecise awareness of the eschatological horizon—the final cause—of the tradition, as vouchsafed by constant and various exposure to the event of revelation in Christ and formation in that revelation's attendant intellectual and moral virtues. Not being myself a saint, I cannot pretend to believe my sense of the truth in this matter particularly sound. And, for just this reason, I also cannot think of this matter in terms of a single correct original version of the tale and its many "false doubles," or of a verifiably correct memory of the tale as opposed to various forms of "misremembering." I prefer to think of the matter, rather, in terms of better and worse enunciations and interpretations within the unfolding historical effects of a revelation that, even in its very first annunciation, always had something of a polyphonic character about it, and that is still moving toward harmonic resolutions yet to be discovered. And to discern which tradition is which, which authentic and which counterfeit, one must rely on any number of ancillary but indispensable intellectual resources, such as coherent metaphysical reasoning and (no less important) simple good taste. I say all of this not on account of some kind of moral tact or agnostic tentativeness on my part. I am altogether happy to denounce what I take to be abominably foolish readings of the tradition, and think it possible to adduce good reasons for doing so. But I also believe that fidelity to the wisdom of the tradition includes a willingness to recover aspects of its truth that have been lost in the contingencies of doctrinal history, by accidental association with streams of reflection that at one time or another were retroactively condemned as forms of apostasy or deviation, in some cases rather unfairly. After all, simply as a matter of critical probity, how can one definitively and impartially distinguish with finality between heretical distortions and legitimate developments of doctrine, when both have often departed with equal abruptness from what preceded them? What is the tradition's phantom reflection and what its true semblance? Who enjoys the privilege of remembering "correctly"? Surely it would be little more than an evasion for the historian of ideas to invoke something like Newman's theory of doctrinal development (that grand exercise in tautologous reasoning). If all tradition, all "orthodoxy," is a tale at once of unbroken continuity and of constant novelty, and of a practice of pious recollection that is also a ruthless revision of the past, surely one must exercise a certain salutary diffidence here. What, for instance, might at first appear at any given moment to be the recrudescence of a heterodox school long ago consigned to the midden of deviant theologies might in fact be only—or, at the very least, *also*—a suppressed but ineradicable element of the tradition rising to the surface once more, perhaps in an unfortunately extreme form. Even if there has been some kind of gnostic return in modernity, then, we might do well to ask what has really prompted it, and whether it might actually be the necessary resurgence of some aspect of the theological imagination whose long absence from Christian consciousness has left a vacancy that nothing else can fill.

Perhaps the best questions to ask of ourselves before even attempting to isolate the true transmission of the tradition from its errant imitations would be: How has our own memory been constituted? What necessary moments of willful forgetfulness does it depend upon? But, then, if we ask these things in earnest, a potentially interminable historical aetiology and reconstruction has been inaugurated. And here yet another specter arises: the disturbing possibility that, within the record of the tradition, no final distinction between the one original true text and the many palimpsests obscuring it can be drawn, simply because the "original" itself is not a discrete, inert object; it is, rather, by its very nature, a dynamic process of change, one not only tolerating, but actually subsisting in, a series of accretions, suppressions, revisions, and renewals. Again, how can we know that the original is not itself only a phantom figure produced solely by the play of simulacra—a haunting absence that must occasionally be concealed by one or another doctrinal compromise, or a haunting ubiquity that perpetually refuses reduction to a single uniform manifestation? Perhaps, when all those opaque or diaphanous layers of historical contingency are stripped away, all that remains is an open question. Perhaps the odyssey back to the one true homeland of the faith is a fantasy, and Ithaca's headland will always lie somewhere just beyond an endlessly receding succession of jetties, bluffs, capes, chersoneses, and the occasional mirage. If nothing else, the one true great Hegelian discovery—the binary mechanisms of conceptual change, the kaleidoscopic flow of ceaseless inversion, the always vital and refractory latency of every principle in its own negation—suggests that this could prove to be the whole story at the last. Perhaps what we deem to be either orthodoxy or heterodoxy—anamnesis or "misremembering," the original or its ghostly double—is entirely determined by our relative appetites for the familiar or the exotic. I do not want to exaggerate my own skepticism on this issue, of course. Again, I believe there are a great many ways of negotiating the ambiguities of the tradition, and of distinguishing between better and worse expressions of its truths. But I do think that there are questions here that one may genuinely pose with regard to a project of historical reconstructions and analytical discriminations like O'Regan's (without for a moment denying its rigor, comprehensiveness, subtlety, or brilliance). At the very least, one might ask where so grand a project of recollection, and so tireless a labor of isolating the true version of the Christian story while exposing its counterfeits, can safely and convincingly come to a halt; one might justly wonder whether, once initiated, the entire enterprise might prove to be, just as a matter of logical consistency, an indefatigable and universal solvent, ultimately dispelling the entire insubstantial pageant, leaving not a rack behind.

So, then, my final question: Can O'Regan enunciate and fully elaborate a systematic set of principles and a clear method for discriminating, wholly in terms of his genealogical and historical project and without any leaps of faith, between the true Christian narrative and its false doubles? Though, really, Yeats phrased the problem far better:

O chestnut tree, great-rooted blossomer,
Are you the leaf, the blossom or the bole?
O body swayed to music, O brightening glance,
How can we know the dancer from the dance?

SIX

The Chiasmus

The Created Supernatural and the Natural Divine

Daz ouge, dä inne ich got sihe, daz ist daz selbe ouge, dä inne
mich got sihet; mîn ouge und gotes ouge daz ist éin ouge und
éin gesiht und éin bekennen und éin minnen.
—Meister Eckhart[1]

I: Transcendental Longing for the Chiasmus

1. Granting the legitimacy and necessity of all the traditional apophatic
restrictions placed upon our language regarding God, we still should not
hesitate to affirm that the irrepressible transcendental desire of any rational nature is to ascend from the indigence of mere phenomenal experience to the boundless richness of a perfect and immediate knowledge
of the wellsprings of all Being. Whatever the limits of our desires and
ambitions as psychological selves or empirical egos may or ought to
be, all our mental intentions and volitional inclinations are embraced
within—and could not exist apart from—a more primordial movement
of the rational will toward its one infinite source and end. This does not
contradict the rule that finite intellects cannot comprehend the infinite

in itself: the apophatic is, in a sense, logically entailed in the very concept of desire for *infinite* knowledge. What we seek, however, is not a quantitative accumulation of all possible "information"; what we seek is not a mere "knowledge about" (ἐπιστήμη)—but rather an immediate acquaintance, a true "knowledge of" (γνῶσις)—Being in its transcendent fullness. This is obvious. No finite terminus of desire could draw the rational will to itself were it not set off against the encompassing infinite horizon of Being in its transcendental perfections. Only thus is anything finite capable of becoming for us an object of recognition, evaluation, and judgment, and so of election, rejection, or indifference. We love the Good, the True, the Beautiful as ultimate objects of what Maximus the Confessor calls our natural will; we love anything finite only as an object illumined by this natural desire and then submitted to the determinations of the "gnomic" or deliberative will. And, but for this "supernatural" illumination, that object would never be visible to the intellect or the will as an object of choice. But for a tacit rational grasp of the supernatural, as the most original movement of our nature, we would be incapable of any explicit rational grasp of the natural. As Nicholas of Cusa says, *"Quod nisi deus esset infinitus, non foret finis desidere"*: "Were God not infinite, he could not be an end for desire." Or, in the words of William Law, "Thy natural senses cannot possess God, or unite thee to Him; nay, thine inward faculties of Understanding, Will and Memory can only reach after God, but cannot be the place of his habitation in thee. But there is a root or depth in thee, from whence all these faculties come forth, as lines from a centre, or as branches from the body of the tree. This depth is called the Centre, the Fund or Bottom of the soul. This depth is the Unity, the Eternity, I had almost said the Infinity of thy soul; for it is so infinite that nothing can satisfy it, or give it any rest but the infinity of God."[2]

2. We know the transcendent end that calls to us before (and after) any concepts we may employ to capture it as something answerable to our gaze and to our will. We know the supernatural first, and the natural only in consequence thereof. Our first "empirical" or "affective" experience of this transcendental vocation comes as that pre-conceptual wonder at the sheer givenness of being, the sheer inexplicability of existence,

that seizes us even in childhood, and that fitfully takes hold of us again and again throughout life in those rare moments when we make an unanticipated and transitory surrender to the mystery of Being's event. In such moments, we experience, in addition to even the commonest object of attention, the mysterious fortuity of its existence, the infinitely irreducible interval of the surfeit of Being over beings. But we also thereby discover an intentional range within ourselves capable of that interval, and so capable of going beyond the finite occasion of experience toward the inexhaustible source of its event, the whole actuality of Being. As we age, of course, we attempt to banish that wonder from our minds, and to master the mystery of Being in comprehensible ideas or projects. But, in its first apprehension, it is an experience of an intimacy with Being's mystery as yet uninterrupted by concepts of the mind or purposes of the will. And what we crave in the deepest reaches of our nature is at once a return to and an advance toward a still higher intimacy with that mystery, one in which again those concepts and purposes can no longer separate us from what calls to us—now, not because they have yet to be formulated, but because they have been exhausted. We seek a wise innocence that knows directly. In the deepest reaches of our thoughts and desires, we seek to become transparent in mind and will to the λόγος of all things.

3. To say this otherwise: It is an axiom of philosophy—one that requires no particular metaphysical commitments—that the *ordo cognoscendi* is the inversion of the *ordo essendi*, and that the *terminus ad quem* of each is the *terminus a quo* of the other. This is obvious from the most minimal conditions of experience. In temporal terms, all causes and their effects are simultaneous, as ancient and mediaeval tradition asserts, even in cases of causes that "arrive" from past or future. In the *ordo essendi*, however, all causes are logically prior to their effects. And in the *ordo cognoscendi* just the reverse is true: all causes are posterior discoveries, preceded by a sheer event that is a phenomenal experience *before* it is an intelligible truth; the event comes first for us, while its causes lie only at the end of the wakened intellect's journey toward a reality that the event has already made manifest, but not yet rendered wholly intelligible. Usually, this axiom is taken merely as an epistemological rule: that, for us,

causes are known only through their effects. It should, however, be taken no less as an ontological law: Being is of necessity disclosure, replete in itself only insofar as it is known to intentional mind, while true knowledge must then be nothing less than a direct participation in Being's most essential actuality. The inverse proportions of these two *ordines* are in fact simply two ways of looking at the inseparable and complementary terms of the single indivisible event of being and knowing.

II: Knowledge and Being as the Chiasmus

4. We are accustomed, here in modernity's evening twilight, to conceive of our knowledge of the world principally as a regime of representation, according to which sensory intuitions are transformed into symbolic images by some kind of neurological and perceptual metabolism, and then subjected to whatever formal conceptual determinations our transcendental apperception and apparatus of perception might permit. The act of knowing, in this scheme, is not situated immediately within Being's own movement of disclosure; conversely, that movement is not immediately situated within the mind's most proper act. Knowledge, then, consists in no more than a kind of cognitive allegory *of* and logical deduction *about* Being, because Being in itself possesses an occult adversity or resistance to being known. All that we experience in experiencing the world, then, is an obscure, logically inexplicable, but unremitting correspondence between mind and world, one whose ontological basis is not a presumed primordial identity between them, but rather something like a pre-established harmony or purely fortuitous synchrony—or inexplicably coherent illusion. The more rational assumption, however, is that so implausible a liaison between absolutely incommensurable spheres of reality is impossible, and that in fact mind and world must belong to one another from the first, as flowing from and continuously participating in a single source that is at once ontological and gnoseological, and in which the ontological and the gnoseological are one and the same.

5. Under the regime of representation, the intelligible is a veil drawn before the abyss of the unintelligible, and the unintelligible is more real

than the intelligible. But what would it really mean to say that something exists that is, of its nature, alien to intelligibility? Can Being and knowing be wholly severed from one another without creating an intolerable contradiction? Could anything truly exist in such a fashion that it could never be either perceived or thought of, even if only in principle? How would such a reality be distinct from absolute nothingness? It certainly seems reasonable to assume that Being must also be manifestation, that real subsistence must also be real disclosure, that to exist is to be perceptible, conceivable, knowable, and that to exist fully is to be manifest to consciousness. So long as any absolute qualitative disproportion remains between Being and knowing, then, Being cannot become manifest, and so *is* not. Being must be intelligible, or even intelligibility itself. The perfectly unintelligible is a logical and ontological contradiction.

6. Being and knowing must, then, coincide in some principle of form. That is, there must be that which is at once ontological and gnoseological in every instance of Being's disclosure to thought. Only in the transcendence of form over the formed—whether the latter be a material substrate or the intentionality of the mind—can there be a place of true indistinction between the being of an object and the knowledge of that object. Only in form—only in the informing cause of both an object's finite existence and the act of understanding that takes that object in—can the secret and most primordial impulse of all philosophy realize its end. Only in form, understood as a real principle of both being and knowing, can ontology and epistemology coincide as a single event of manifestation, of Being's disclosure, which is to say also, of the full existence of what is made manifest. The deepest and most original vocation animating philosophy is the prospect of an ideal ascent to that juncture—that chiastic point where the orders of Being and of knowing are inverted each into the other, in a singular event of disclosure—where our evening knowledge will be consummated in the morning knowledge of God, and yield to it, so that we might at last know even as we are known.

7. Once again, the unthinkable—the impossible—is that the phenomenal, eidetic, Platonic order of essences that we necessarily inhabit as rational spirit is not the real order of Being as such, and not even its epiphenomenal expression (because in itself that reality *expresses* nothing at

all), but rather is only the representing faculty's useful dissemblance of Being's utter opacity. Being, then, would be a pure enigma, the unintelligible occasion of an intelligibility whose coherence lies in its illusoriness. But then, would not the very coherence of the illusion be itself something of a miracle? A kind of fortuitously continuous concomitant of that inexpressive reality, an inexplicably correlated or synchronous negation? At its most debased, this view of things becomes the materialist superstition that all that *really* exists is some hyper-phenomenal (or hypo-phenomenal) realm of pure quantifiable extension, force, and mass, while the glorious, glamorous veil of phenomenal experience is nothing but the product of an illusory consciousness deluded into thinking it is really experiencing what is in fact an illusory world.

III: Trinity and Creation as the Chiasmus

8. A metaphysical boundary was crossed—albeit invisibly, even inadvertently—with the Trinitarian dogmatic definitions of the fourth century and their *sequelae*, and thus a new path for Christian thought was opened: a wholly ontological way of speculation, as opposed to a metaphysics of pure "hierarchy within totality," in which an implicit univocity of being reduced God to the supreme "existent" merely prior to and more original than all subsequent and dependent existents, at the inaccessible apex of the hierarchy of things that are. Once it had become impossible to conceive of the processions of the divine Persons as a progressive diminishment of the paternal origin as an accommodation to lower reality, or to conceive of the created order as located simply at the termination of that continuum, creation came to seem in one sense detached from the *taxis* of the divine; much more radically, however, it was revealed as being "located" nowhere but *within* the very life of God *as* God. Its existence, its constitution, its form—none of this could be seen as merely a remote effect of divine power; all of it had to be seen as a revelation of the divine actuality, as theophany; all of it came to be seen as the immediate action of God as Spirit, through the Logos, who is the perfect reflection of the Father. What causes creation to be, to have form, to live is nothing other than a direct participation in that order of rela-

tions by which God is God. And yet, as far as theological consciousness was at first aware, the final resolution of the debate was determined by soteriology: only by way of the co-equality of the divine hypostases was it possible coherently to maintain that the Spirit, in conforming creatures to the incarnate Son, truly joins them to the eternal Father, and thereby truly deifies them. Still, this meant that the Logos, as understood in light of the Nicene settlement, is not a reduced manifestation of a God who, in his fullness, is simply beyond all manifestation. Rather, the Logos is the eternal reality of God's manifestation of his own essence to himself, and therefore the eternal act whereby God is God. This perfectly co-equal convertibility of God with his own manifestation of himself to himself is God's own act of self-knowledge and self-love in the mystery of his transcendent life. Thus his being is an infinite intelligibility; even his hiddenness—his transcendence—is always already manifestation too. This movement of infinite disclosure is nothing less than his "essence" as God. As Gregory of Nyssa says, apart from his Son, the Father would have no light, truth, wisdom, life, holiness, or power;[3] the eternal "mirroring" of the Father in the Son is that one original act of knowledge in which each of the Persons shares; the Only Begotten, says Gregory, who dwells in the Father, sees the Father in himself, while the Spirit searches out the deeps of God.[4] God himself is an eternal play of the invisible and the visible, the hidden Father made luminously manifest in the infinite icon of his beauty, God "speculating" upon himself by way of his absolute self-giving in the other. Or, as Augustine says, the co-equal Son is an image that perfectly fills the measure of the Father imaged in him, and the beauty of this perfect correspondence eventuates in that fruition, love, rejoicing, delight, felicity, and beatitude that is the Holy Spirit, who in turn fills all creatures with his own bounty; "therefore those three are seen to be mutually determined, and are in themselves infinite."[5]

9. It is from this original "circle of glory"[6] that the logic of created being unfolds: a specular ontology, according to which creation is constituted as simply another inflection of an infinite light, receiving God's effulgence as that primordial gift that completes itself in summoning its own return into existence. Creation *is* only as the answer of light to light, a

created participation in the self-donating movement of the Trinity, existing solely as the manifestation—the reflection—of the splendor of a God whose own being is manifestation, recognition, and delight.

10. Inasmuch as Being must be convertible with manifestation or intelligibility, then the God who is also always Logos is also eternal Being: not *a* being, that is, but transcendent Being, beyond all finite existence. Here, at last, is a Christian rationality of God as "*esse subsistens*," or Being in itself, which is to say an entirely Trinitarian rationality.

11. At the same time, a question was implicitly raised and secretly incubated by Christian tradition, one that could occasionally be glimpsed in certain of the more daring speculative schemes of premodern Christianity (the thought of Maximus the Confessor, the system of John Scotus Eriugena, certain fugitive formulations in Nicholas of Cusa), but that for the most part remained unspoken: If God's eternal being as God is his knowledge of his own essence in the "infinite mirror" of the Logos and the consummation of this act of knowing in the infinite satisfaction of the Spirit—and if, therefore, there is no surfeit of the Father over the Son and Spirit, no yet-more-hidden transcendence of the Father grasped by himself alone, by way of some kind of "superintellection" beyond manifestation and recognition—and if God is then an infinite act of intelligibility who knows himself in and through the manifestation of himself to himself—how then can the event of God's eternal self-knowledge be discriminated from God's eternal knowledge of creation in his Logos, or that knowledge of creation from his eternal being *as* God? Surely the temporal is, from the perspective of the finite, contingent. But, from the perspective of the eternal life of God, God's manifestation of himself to himself is never without his manifestation in creation, and so creation is eternally present within the eternal act whereby God is God. Obscurely, perhaps, and at first entirely subliminally, but nonetheless inevitably, the possibility of something like the Hegelian deduction is implicit as an inevitable moment in Christian reflection—one to be either ultimately affirmed or ultimately rejected or ultimately qualified, but not to be avoided. What we understand to be a *particular* history of revelation depends upon and discloses the reality

of a universal history that belongs from everlasting to the shape of the divine life. If indeed the logic of the Nicene settlement was determined principally by the demands of soteriology, it seems difficult to avoid the ultimate conclusion that the *ordo salutis* and the *ordo entis* are one and the same, and that all that exists has its being as God's knowledge of himself in his Logos. The union of creation with God is both the most ultimate and most original of creaturely truths; divinization, though it be the consummation of creation in time, is the beginning of creation in eternity, and it can be neither without being the other. And nothing can exist that is not always already, in eternity, divinized, plunged ecstatically into the fire of the divine life.

12. Inasmuch as God is not a finite being, in whom possibility exceeds actuality, but is infinitely actual, and is in fact the eternal act of all things actual, in him there is no meaningful modal distinction between freedom and necessity. He is the supereminent fullness of all that is, and his freedom is the unhindered actuality of being who he is. Therefore his "election" of himself in the Son in the Spirit's light is always also the eternal reality of his election of himself in all that is contained in the Logos, including the entirety of creation and history. The drama of creation and salvation is not a distant analogy of the divine life, and the presence of the *taxis* of the Trinity right within the dynamism of creaturely divinization is not merely a secondary effect of the eternal divine *taxis*. Neither is it something external to the divine identity, nor is it the exhaustion of divine emanation in some *kenoma* outside of the divine life. However inviolable and absolute the analogical interval between God and creation may be, it cannot be an interval merely of accidental and extrinsic relatedness between two separate *things*. Our being in God and God's being in us are both also and more originally God's being as God. And so nothing can be excluded from that return of all things joyously to their source and yet really exist, any more than God could be only one part of a larger realm of actuality. Nothing can exist in history that is not always already redeemed and divinized in eternity. All things are created in their last end, and if they were not already fully reconciled to God and in full spiritual and ontological union with him they would never come into existence. Created spirits exist because they are, from everlasting, gods in God. (*Vide infra.*)

IV: The Chiasmus of the Spirit (1)

13. It would be difficult to enumerate with certainty all the places in Paul's authentic epistles in which he speaks of "spirit" in so ambiguous a way that it is impossible to tell whether he means God's or ours. Or perhaps it would be more accurate to say that there are an enormous number of passages in which it seems plausible that he means both at once, or sees no need to specify that he means the one rather than the other—because, that is, he is speaking about that *one* reality that is simultaneously God's eternal Spirit and also the spirit that abides in us as our innermost selves, breathed into us by God in the beginning of days. See, for example, Romans 5:5; 7:6; 8:2–16; 8:23–27; 9:1; 14:7; 1 Corinthians 2:4; 2:10–16; 3:16; 6:17; 14:2; 14:14–16; 2 Corinthians 4:13; 6:6; Galatians 3:2–5; 4:29; 5:5; 5:16–26; 6:8; Philippians 1:27; 2:1; and so forth. And, of course, such moments are found not only in the authentic epistles. Translations often dissemble the amphibology, and in so doing also perhaps conceal what is most astonishing and mysterious and essential to Paul's vision. But surely this ambiguity is entirely appropriate: the final terminus of the divine descent—the Spirit who descends from the Father and by way of the Son to sanctify creatures—is also the initiation of the creaturely ascent—the process of sanctification that raises the creature up in the Spirit, through the Son, to be joined to the Father. Here, just as with the order of Being and knowing, so too is the order of *kenosis* and *plerosis* one and the same action, both divine and created, as viewed from inverse perspectives. We are, from the moment when we are called from nonbeing, spirit becoming Spirit; God is, from everlasting, Spirit disclosing himself in the creation of spiritual beings and the continuous divinization of every spirit that he has breathed forth in breathing himself. And so, in that chiastic inversion of divine and created spiritual life, where God's creating and sanctifying Spirit is also the spirit breathed into the clay from which we are formed, creating the living soul roused from nothingness and drawn into the infinite, there is a place of indistinction that is at once the beginning and the end of both creation and salvation.

14. Romans 8:11 is intelligible only as the confirmation of Genesis 2:7 (as well as of, in another way, Ecclesiastes 12:7). Irenaeus is an especially interesting witness to this truth, in part because he appears to have grasped it with an altogether innocent sense of its obvious orthodoxy, which in his time and place was apparently largely uncontroversial. "If one subtracts the flesh's substance (which is to say, the fashioned clay) and reflects on only the naked spirit, what remains is not 'the spiritual man' but only 'a man's spirit' or 'God's spirit.' Yet, when this spirit is blended with the soul and joined to the fashioned clay, what arises, by the grace of the spirit's outpouring, is a spiritual and complete man, and it is he, the complete man, who has been created in the image and likeness of God."[7] And, of course: "Where there is the Father's Spirit, there is a living human being."[8] Strictly speaking, then, while there are such things as "spiritual creatures," there really is no such thing as "created spirit." By a pardonable and necessary solecism, we speak of "created spirits" or of "*a* created spirit" when we wish to identify discrete hypostases—that is, finite, "ensouled" and embodied participants in the breath of the Father—but that remains, at most, a convenient *façon de parler.*

15. According to Gregory of Nyssa, when our nature draws near to Christ, it becomes beautiful with the reflection of his beauty.[9] For the soul is a kind of "free and living mirror" that, in gazing upon the face of its lover the Logos, is adorned with his comeliness;[10] by looking at him, one becomes what he is.[11] But the Logos is also the blinding sun that cannot be looked at directly, and that can be glimpsed only in its image: the soul that mirrors its beauty in her own purity.[12] Finite creatures, moreover, can become mirrors of the infinite only because the infinite, within itself, is entirely mirroring of itself—in that the Father's incomprehensible majesty is eternally united to the co-equal "splendor of his glory," his "form" and "impress," in seeing whom one has seen the Father. We can become images of God that shine with his beauty because the Father always has his image in his Son, bright with the light of his Spirit, and so is never without form and loveliness.[13] There is, moreover, a very particular sense in which the light of the Spirit, for Gregory, is that perfecting radiance, that fullness of glory, that "completes" the unity of

the godhead:[14] when Christ prays in John 17, says Gregory, that his disciples might be one—even as he and his Father are one and indwell one another—and then affirms that the glory that the Father has given him he has given them, he is speaking of the gift of the Holy Spirit; indeed, that glory *is* the Spirit, the glory that the Son had with the Father before the world was made,[15] the "bond of peace" or "bond of unity" (so like the Augustinian *vinculum caritatis*) by which Father and Son dwell in one another, and by which we dwell in God when the Son breathes the Spirit forth upon us.[16] There is, in the Trinitarian life, a "revolving circle of glory, from like to like,"[17] and it is into this that the Spirit draws us,[18] so that by being refashioned after and within the Trinitarian ordering of self-outpouring light we are assimilated to God. Thus the "course" of glory in the Godhead—the *taxis* of the divine being—impresses its own reflex in our specular natures, almost under the form of an inversion of the light (as is proper for a mirror), so that God's own loving "return" to himself is our integration into him. Everything—being, power, creation,[19] holiness, love, truth, faith[20]—flows from the Father, through the Son, to the Spirit, and is restored by the Spirit, through the Son, to the Father.

16. One cannot say that Jesus is Lord, claims Gregory, or mount up in thought to the Son or, through him, to the Father, except in the Holy Spirit.[21] The hypostasis of the Father can be grasped only in its impress (χαρακτήρ), the unique Son, and none can approach the Son unless the light of the Holy Spirit illuminates his or her mind.[22] And that place where the light of the Spirit and the mirror of the soul are one, and where a moment of indistinction is necessarily achieved, is also the point where a chiasmus of the Trinitarian *taxis* occurs. A mirror inverts the light that touches it, and in a sense ascends to the source of that light in the very act of reflecting the order of its descent. As the mind journeys inward toward the height of its spiritual awareness of God it also journeys outward and upward to the paternal source of all. The mirror of the soul is that ideal surface where two depths are reconciled, or where one depth creates another: the infinite light of God, flowing from the Father, through the Son, to the Spirit, and its "specular" repetition in the soul's ascent from its more "exterior" to its more "interior" aspects, repeating

in the realm of created finitude the infinite's play of hiddenness and manifestation. The three marks of the Christian life, says Gregory, appear in practice, word (λόγος), and thought (ἐνθύμιον); the principle (ἀρχικώτερον) of all three is thought, for mind (διάνοια) is that original source (ἀρχή) that then manifests itself in speech, while practice comes third and puts mind and word into action.[23] Inasmuch as the soul's principle, the mind, expresses itself in word and act, moving from full hiddenness to open disclosure, just so the Spirit, meeting spiritual creatures in their fleshly acts and words, conducts the Trinitarian glory "upward" into their thinking, refashioning them so that their depths are ever more conformed to the brightening surfaces of their natures, making their return to themselves simultaneously both the reflection of God's return to himself within his eternal circle of glory and their own real ascent out of themselves—out of their creaturely insubstantiality—into his infinity.

17. God's Spirit is the fullness of the divine life, while the spirit of the creature has its beginning and its existence only in the return of that fullness to its fountainhead. The creature's ascent to God is already situated within God's eternal return to himself, as a participating modality of God's *kenosis* and *plerosis*, both in the *exitus* and *reditus* of creation and in the Trinitarian processions. If the divine Spirit is the consummation in delight of the Father's knowledge of himself in the Son, so finite spirit exists as having been ever called to seek the unity of the Logos and the Father—of intelligibility and Being—in the satiety of that very same eternal bond of love or bond of glory.

V: The Chiasmus of the Son

18. For Christian thought, the event of Christ—the event of the Son in time—is the rational structure of all history, cosmic and human. It is in this event that the eternal and the temporal are conjoined as a single and indivisible unity. And this is a point at once of convergence and of divergence. This is the chiasmus at the center of creation, the very place where creation occurs as an eternal act of God. The event presupposes—and so calls into being—its entire historical past and entire historical future.

It also presupposes its own universality, both as a concrete historical datum and as an inexhaustible transhistorical symbol. For this reason, there can be no meaningful separation between history as such and some special, magically separate diegetic exception to the larger narrative called "salvation history." The very particularity of the event is the chiastic point of indistinction wherein all things "consist," and no single tradition can possibly unfold the universal content of that infinitely condensed juncture in any but a partial way. There can be only differing historical modalities whereby creatures respond to the event that brings all things into being (even when much or all of that event as a historical datum is formally unknown to them): different languages, different traditions, different religions, and so forth, but all of them always existing as responses and approaches to the God who pours himself forth in creation, even to the point of identity with one historical man, and who draws all creation out of nothingness to himself, even to the point of identity with the "all in all."

19. For this reason, incidentally, the religion historically called "Christianity" is not a "truth" that exists among and in competition with "false" non-Christian religions. "Christianity," in fact—which is not really one thing, in any event, but only a loose designation for a diverse set of beliefs and practices and cultural forms and numerous often incongruous *religions*, comprised within a single but nonetheless porous hermeneutical and historical "set"—is only one limited trajectory within history's universal narrative of divine incarnation and creaturely deification, superior in some ways to alternative trajectories, vastly inferior in many others. (A strictly Reformed theology of, say, penal substitutionary atonement is infinitely more remote from the Logos who has become incarnate in created nature and history than is, for instance, the bodhisattva ideal unfolded in the *Lotus Sutra* and the *Bodhicaryavatara*; indeed, the latter in some very real sense attests, under the veil of the unfamiliar, to the truth made present in Christ, while the former is totally antithetical to that truth and therefore pure falsehood. A manualist Thomist "two-tier" understanding of the relation between the supernatural and the natural, or between the divine and the created, with its associated concept of *natura pura*, is so contrary to everything proper to the narrative of divine incarnation and creaturely divinization that it

is immeasurably more irreconcilable with any truth revealed in Christ than is the metaphysics of classical Vedanta, in either its *Advaita* or *Vishishtadvaita* form. Sri Ramakrishna's understanding of the nature of an *avatara* is truer to the gospel than is Calvin's bifurcated Christology. And so on.) And the concrete community of the church—which is merely a first-fruits of the harvest of the new creation, an earnest of a Kingdom both already here and also yet to appear—is at once more particular and more universal than any religion (including any or all of the Christian religions); and the invisible church is at once more original, more ultimate, and more comprehensive than the visible—so much so that in its final end it is perfectly coterminous, albeit under the aspect of the created, with the God who is "all in all." The church is simply a corporate and historical expression of Christ's affirmation that "You are gods." What is true of him is true of us, even though we exist as the created (rather than uncreated) subjects of that truth, and in our created (rather than uncreated, which is to say inmost) nature *participate* in that godhead rather than *impart* it. Still, even so, there is an "infinite destiny" implicit in that created experience: that final indistinction, when "I shall know even as I am known."

20. But for this union of divine and human, humanity would have no existence, since it would have no final cause. In the incarnate Logos, in the reconciliation of God and creation effected by the hypostatic union of the uncreated and created, the divine humanity that is the premise of creation is perfectly realized; and, in constituting the end toward which creation is oriented and in which it is established, this premise brings humanity into being *solely* as a mode of participation in the divine. In this perfect coincidence of the wholly eternal and wholly historical, the natural and constitutive transparency of humanity to God finds not only its axis, but the whole rationale of creation. This is why it is impossible to understand divine incarnation as merely a consequence of creaturely sin. There could be no creation at all but for the humanity of God and divinity of human beings; there could be no world but for the historical and cosmic achievement of that union in the event of incarnation, which is always already the perfection of deification. The infralapsarian logic of creation and divine incarnation that one finds in Thomas, for instance—which cannot even provide a coherent account of why God creates *this*

world rather than some other, or of how in doing so he is not reduced to a voluntarist subject arbitrarily selecting from among an infinity of possible worlds, any of which is equally incapable of expressing the infinity of his goodness—is to be rejected without remainder. Only an understanding of creation as grounded in the event of Christ—only an understanding of this world as the one world of Christ—can make sense at once of the gratuity and of the rationality of creation. And that, of course, allows for only a supralapsarian theology of incarnation and deification.

21. It is the "ever greater" transcendence of the divine over the finite that lifts the doctrine of the incarnation out of the realm of myth; for it marks the difference between the divine and the human as an infinite qualitative distance, and as such makes intelligible the claim that there is no conflict or rivalry between Christ's divinity and his humanity. Thus it is that the latter participates in the former so naturally that the one person of the Son can be both fully divine and fully human at once. If the difference between God and humanity were a merely quantifiable difference between extrinsically related beings, the incarnation would be a real change in one or both natures, an amalgamation or synthesis; but then Christ would be not the God-man, but a monstrosity, a hybrid of natures that, in themselves, would remain opposed and unreconciled. Since, however, the difference between the divine and the human is really an infinite qualitative difference, the hypostatic union involves no contradiction, alienation, or change in the divine Son. Since the difference between God and creation is the difference between Being and created beings, Christ is not an irresoluble paradox fixed within the heart of faith, or an accommodation between two different kinds of "thing"; in his one person—both God and a man—there is neither any diminishment of his divinity nor any violation of the integrity of his humanity. In a sense, in Christ one sees the "analogy of Being" with utter clarity: that is, one glimpses at once both the perfect ontological interval of divine transcendence and also the perfect fittingness of the divine image to its archetype. For the perfect man is also God of God: not a fabulous demigod, but human in the fullest sense because divine in the fullest sense.

22. In Christ one also sees the chiasmus of the divine and the created in its most pellucid purity. All things created are wholly contained from eternity—in their principles and in their actuality—within the Logos who is the Father's co-equal image, and so are eternally loved and redeemed and deified within the Father's utterance of and delight in the whole of the divine essence. And, no less truly, the Logos is wholly contained—as a historical event and as the fullest exemplary instance of created nature—within the totality of creation. All created things are contained within the scope of the incarnation, so much so that one must say that creation *is* the incarnation in the fullness of all its necessary historical and natural dimensions. And hence the incarnate Logos is that critical juncture wherein the whole of the created order consists as one coherent act of God expressing himself "beyond" himself. And this because that "beyond" is always already contained within the order of knowledge and love that is the divine life.

23. Hence the inseparability of the Christ of the synoptic gospels from the Johannine Christ: the simultaneity and identity, that is, of the way of ascent and the way of descent, of the summing up of humanity in its perfect transparency to God and the revelation of God by his perfect descent into an intrinsically theophanic humanity. It is in the synoptic gospels that the Father is most definitely "the invisible of the Son," behind the veil of the messianic secret and of the flesh of Israel, while it is in the fourth gospel that the Son is most radiantly "the visible of the Father" in the light of the resurrection.[24] But he can be seen truly only under both aspects at once. Christ is, at one and the same time and in the very same life and actions, *both* the prophet proclaiming the Kingdom, pronouncing the displeasure of God upon the wealthy, the cruel, the violent, the hypocritical, and all who neglect mercy, always situated within human history and culture and moving inexorably toward the eminently human destiny of the cross, and thereby in every moment of his story expressing the longing of creation for its God—*and also* the divine savior who descends into this cosmos from the divine Aeon as a conqueror, in perfect contrariety to the Archon and archons of this age and to the logic of fallen history, constituting in his person the impenetrable enigma of the eternal within time, the light of judgment by which

all secret things are exposed, the truth that transcends every historical instant, every place, every limited association, the one whose every human action and word is always already pervaded and transfigured by the eschatological light of the accomplished resurrection, of the Last Day and the Age to Come, and of the divine "destiny" of eternal life in the Aeon "above." Christ is, as the historical personage Jesus of Nazareth, *both* the historical *concretissimum* of creation's union with God, a man of his time and place given over entirely in his every word and deed to the God whose Kingdom will come in history, a man awaiting and prophesying (to the point ultimately of coinciding in his own person with) the figure of the Son of Man who brings about the final judgment upon fallen history—*and is also*, as the eternal Logos, the *universale* of God's eternal condescension toward creatures, the Heavenly Man or Man from Above who has seen what no person born from below can see until that person has been reborn "from Above" in him, the one who pours himself out entirely in (to the point of perfect identity with) the suffering servant who endures this world's judgment and bears the consequences of that judgment even unto death. He is the judge who endures the judgment of history in our place; he is the judged who will judge all of history. He is *both* the anarchist and communist rebel and agitator and religious reformer, the peasant or child of the despised artisanal class who has no place to lay his head, who is constantly struggling against the injustice and cruelty of all the orders of power and privilege governing this world, even though he is defenseless against them in his flesh—*and also* the Lord and king of invincible power, overthrowing the celestial rulers and thrones and dominions and principalities, shattering the household of Hades, in himself the presence of the Kingdom *now*, the one who rests his head forever on the breast of the Father and who is so mighty that no one can take his life from him: for he alone both freely lays it down and takes it up again.

VI: The Chiasmus of the Father

24. The God who *is* brings into union with himself the gods who are always coming to be, and thereby brings creation into existence and leads

it to its consummation wholly *within* the Father's expression of himself in the Son and return to himself in the Spirit. Surely Hegel is to be commended for recognizing with such acuity that the whole rationality of Christian confession requires that nothing in nature or history can be simply extrinsic to this movement of the Father's "achievement" of his own essence in the divine life. Our creation—our theogony—must be the created realization of the shape of that perichoretic plenitude. Even so, God becoming human and humanity becoming God is *not* God becoming God. Rather, the creature's divinization is the creaturely dimension of a divine fullness that, in its infinity of powers, must also express itself in just such a dimension. The infinite fullness of divine being, in that it is the fullness of self-outpouring and self-receiving love, necessarily calls into being that which is other than itself to be included within that divine life; otherwise that love would not be the perfect fullness that it is. But the ordering of the analogical interval between the divine fullness and creation's unending advance into that fullness—between *esse ipsum* and existence *in fieri*—cannot be reversed.

25. All too often, this is obscured in theological discourse by such questions as whether we are obliged to think of creation either as a free act of God's sovereign will or as a product of some necessity incumbent on his will. But this is a false dilemma. God is not a finite being in whom the distinction of freedom from necessity has any meaning. Perfect freedom is the unhindered realization of a nature in its proper end; and God's infinite freedom is the eternal fulfillment of the divine nature in the divine life. Needless to say, for any finite rational being, since its essence is not identical with its existence, any movement toward the realization of its nature is attended by the shadows of unrealized possibilities, and entails deliberative liberty with regard to proximate ends. This, though, is a condition not of freedom as such, but only of finitude. Every decision of the finite will is a collapse of indeterminate potentiality into determinate actuality, and therefore the reduction of limitless possibilities to the bare singularity of one reality. Yet that prior realm of possibility exists only because there is an inexhaustible wellspring of more original and transcendent actuality sustaining it. God, by contrast, simply *is* that actuality, in all its supereminent fullness: infinite Being,

the source of every act of being. As such, he is infinitely free precisely because nothing can inhibit or limit the perfect realization of his nature, and thus, as Maximus says, he possesses no gnomic will; for God, deliberative liberty—any "could have been otherwise," any arbitrary decision among opposed possibilities—would be an impossible defect of his freedom. God does not require the indeterminacy of the possible in order to be free because he is not some particular determination of Being, some finite reduction of potency to act; he is instead that infinite actuality upon which all ontic possibility depends. And in the calculus of the infinite, any tension between freedom and necessity simply disappears; there is no problem to be resolved because, in regard to the transcendent and infinite fullness of all Being, the distinction is meaningless. God is not a being choosing his nature from among a range of options; he simply is reality as such. And it is only insofar as God is not a being defined by possibility, and is hence infinitely free, that creation inevitably follows from who he is. This in no way alters the truth that creation, in itself, "might not have been," so long as this claim is understood as a modal definition, a statement of ontological contingency, a recognition that creation receives its being from beyond itself and so has no necessity intrinsic to itself.

26. In one sense, it is not in any failure to elevate actuality over potentiality that Hegel departs from classical theological precedent; it may be that the Concept wants for nothing in its Aristotelian unity of initial and final causality. But an ambiguity arises—for some a scandal, for others a source of fascination—in the dynamism of formal and material causality by which that unity is translated into the living knowledge of Spirit. It is tempting to presume (though perhaps impossible to prove with absolute certainty) that the eternal *Begriff* would not suffer the probations of the negative in its historical and natural diremption if there were not, also somehow logically prior to the rational mechanism of dialectic and the epic of *Geist*, some ground of indeterminacy that is a kind of spontaneity, a kind of willing without rationale that becomes rational only in the dialectic and that would otherwise remain an unresolved aporia within (or beyond) the *Begriff* in its eternity. To the degree that *Geist* is truly *accomplished* in the processes of negation, rather than

merely expressed as the living manifestation of an eternal reality already replete in its infinite satiety, to that very degree there appears to be a substrate of the indeterminate not only in creation, but in the eternal "repose" of the Concept. And to say that Spirit is achieved in the negations of the finite is very different from saying that the finite is consummated in the eternal finality of Spirit. In the former case, the violence of nature and history is in some way constitutive of the eternal identity of the divine, and necessarily so; in the latter case, the eternal descent of God toward the creatures he calls into being from nothingness is simply his sovereign liberation of creatures from the darkness of nonbeing, while the violence of finite existence is the recalcitrant residue of that nothingness in its reluctant patiency before the gift of being. In the former case, even the divine must "become" by virtue of a (qualified but real) reduction of potency to act, even if the totality of this process is always already virtually contained in the unexplicated eternity of the Concept; in the latter, all possibility subsists only in the gift of being, which is freely imparted from an eternal wellspring of *actus purus* that is always already absolved of, triumphant over, and in no need of the negative—God as *esse subsistens*, the infinite perfection and simple unity of essence and existence, who imparts being to creatures who are a dynamic synthesis of essence and existence. Surely, the latter picture enjoys the advantage over the former of not mistaking the hell of this fallen world for something proper to the essence of the divine.

27. In the Father, again, there can be no meaningful distinction between freedom and necessity, for there can be nothing extrinsic to or incumbent upon the infinite fullness of Being that God freely and necessarily is, or beyond the infinite fulfillment of the Spirit that the Father freely and necessarily achieves. But even in finite creatures this distinction is arguably accidental only, and ultimately more formal than real. From the perspective of the time of death, *chronos* in its linear movement from beginning to end, the vagrancies of the gnomic faculty and of rational liberty are part of fallen consciousness attempting to recover from a tragedy. The vocation of rational freedom is, so to speak, to gather up the sparks of the *Shekinah* that were lost in the breaking of the vessels, or to aid in the rescue of the lost Sophia; spirit (*neshamah*) is always

called to a homeland that belonged to it before it ever "entered" this world (this being the indubitable truth preserved in "gnosticism"); and yet that homeland was never lost or forsaken in any chronological past, some moment "before" sublunary time as one event in a sequence of discrete events. The fall is a decline from the eternal end in which the creature was created, from which every spiritual creature has departed in failing to embrace its only possible last end within the conditions of time. But even this is possible only by virtue of that which remains forever unfallen within the creature: the natural will that longs and seeks only its own divine fulfillment, the transcendental ecstasy of every spirit in its quest to be united to its source and end—to be embraced within the eternal Logos and thereby translated into union with the fountainhead of all that is, the Father. But all gnomic and all natural movements of the will must alike terminate as one in the divine nature, for all are set free from nonbeing and called to that infinite destiny within the Father's own return to himself in the Trinitarian "circle of glory."

28. To say that God *is* but also *shall be* "all in all" is to say that his eternal act of being God includes within itself his act of being God within the not-God. No dimension of the divine fullness can be lacking, even the dimension of that fullness expressing itself "beyond" itself. The creation, redemption, and deification of rational creation, the restoration and transfiguration of material creation, the whole of God's action within created time—all of it is the created expression of the uncreated in its transcendence even of the division between transcendent and immanent. This is the necessary amphibology of the One: possessing as it must all possibility as actuality in perfect simplicity, it contains within the inner actuality of the divine plenitude even the possibility of creation's relation to its creator *as wholly other*. And God's very perfection and self-sufficiency entail that he express himself as this other even though he can never be "another thing" (*aliud*): for that real possibility cannot be lacking from the simplicity of the divine actuality. Thus the infinite qualitative disproportion between the coincidence of essence and existence in God and the perpetual dynamic synthesis of essence and existence in creatures is simply another inflection and expressive modality of God's life: the Father's co-equal expression in the Son and infinite delight in the Spirit.

VII: The Chiasmus of the Spirit (2)

29. When Paul describes (Romans 14:11; Philippians 2:11) creation's final acclamation of God's majesty in the Age to Come by borrowing the Septuagint's version of Isaiah 45:23, where the Hebrew תִּשָּׁבַע (*tiššāḇaʿ*) is rendered as "ἐξομολογήσεται," he is also describing the moment in which all of creation is called into being. That act of "grateful praise" or "joyous confession" (ἐξομολόγησις) at the end of days is nothing less than the creature's original response to the call that, in the beginning of days, draws all things into being out of nothingness. It is the creature's participation in God's eternal return to himself within the divine life itself and within his *exitus* and *reditus* in creatures. All things are created in their last end, and spiritual creatures possessed of reason and freedom exist only to the degree that they fully assent to and delight in the end that summons them from the night of nothingness. Here, the disproportion and qualitative difference between the eternal and the temporal must be observed with absolute exactitude. The eternal reality of all things is, from the perspective of time, an end to be attained; but, were that end not eternally always so, no finite creature would exist. This is especially so for spiritual creatures, whose very existence *as* spirit can be nothing other than an insatiable intentionality toward the whole of divine being. The final cause of all things that come into being is the whole reality of the created, in its accomplished and so original plenitude. The spiritual life is nothing more than a constant labor to remember our last end by looking forward to our first beginning. The final ἐξομολόγησις of creation is nothing less than its eternal assent to be, its original answer to God's call, its joyous acceptance of the gift of being, and therefore its full moral and spiritual commitment to existence as a wholly contingent manifestation of the divine life in its absoluteness.

30. Every free act—and God's act is freedom as such—is a purposive work accomplished in and by its final cause. God's own goodness—his own essence—is of course the only end of his eternal act of being God, wherein all created actualities subsist by participation. The final cause of all is the initial impulse on which all else is contingent; and in God, whose will is indefectible, his *fiat* in creation is the eternal reality of

creation always already united to him, transfigured, and freely and joyously confessing the God who is all in all. Thus, for instance, Gregory
of Nyssa takes the first creation account in Genesis as referring to the
Primal Human Being, who is the whole plenitude of all men and women
joined to one another and to Christ as their head in eternity, but who in
time exists only as an eschatological terminus toward which all things
are tending. *Sub specie aeternitatis*, creation exists only as glorified,
deified, united to God. *In fieri*, it exists only as moving from nonbeing
and toward that consummation. As Irenaeus says, "*Gloria dei est vivens
homo, vita autem hominis visio dei.*"[25]

31. Sergei Bulgakov understood this perhaps better than any other modern theologian, or at least with greater and more unflagging rigor. At
times, admittedly, he expressed the insight somewhat obscurely (as did
Origen before him), and so it is easy to fail to see how thoroughly he presumes that the logic of eternity entails not only the affirmation of an
"eschatological beginning" for all creatures, but an affirmation also of
that beginning as creation's final free spiritual assent to existence. For
Bulgakov, humanity's spiritual nature is already divine in its very origin;
each human being is from the first a created god who exists as a creature
only in forever being deified, in an infinite ascent into God.[26] But he
also—in a formulation that seems calculated to offend against logic and
piety alike, but that cannot fail to be in some sense true if there really
are such things as spiritual creatures—speaks of human beings as participating in their own origination from nothingness. The spiritual "I,"
in being created, is an I who has been asked to consent to its creation.[27]
And only by this primordial assent does humanity in its eternal "multi-
hypostatic" reality—as the eternal Adam of the first creation—freely
receive its being from its creator: and this even though that assent becomes, on the threshold between the heavenly Aeon and time, a recapitulation of the Fall, an individuating acceptance of entry into the world
under the burden of sin, such that every soul is answerable for and somehow always remembers that original transgression.[28] In that moment, the
spiritual creature concurs in its own creation, and God hands the creature over to its own free self-determination.[29] Here, naturally, the language of past and future can devolve all too easily into a mythology of

individual guilt historically "prior" to any person's actual life; but, of course, there was no fall "back then" in historical time, either for the race or for the individual. Rather, the Fall "happened" only as belonging to the temporal unfolding of that eternal assent. It "happened"—or, rather, is happening—only as the lingering resistance of nothingness to that final joyous confession, the diminishing residue of the creature's emergence *ex nihilo*. For no creature can exist *as spirit* in God except under the condition of having arisen from nothingness in order to grow into his or her last end. That passage from nothingness into the infinite, which is always a free intentionality toward a final cause, is the very structure of created spiritual beings. They could not be spirit otherwise. Any temporal origin *in medias res*, as it were, would rest upon an established and extrinsically imposed *fundamentum inconcussum*, a substratum of the unfree, immutably "posited" prior to any free intention.

32. Here, the logic implicit in Bulgakov's re-Christianization of Fichte seems almost an inevitability for any coherent account of spiritual creation. Finite spirit is, as spirit, always also a self-positing "I," for both better and worse. And it is only as such an "I" that any free spiritual being could be created by God. God cannot create a free rational creature unless that creature is already free in being created—which is to say, unless that creature has freely consented to its own creation, and unless that consent is truly constitutive of the act of its creation. And so, then, it must also be true that no creature can exist *as spirit* except by its free acceptance of the invitation to arise from nothingness, and by intending itself in intending its final cause. Spirit exists as an act of assent to the Father and, in that assent, an act of complete acceptance of the gift of being. Though whatever is created must be created in its last end, still spiritual existence is possible only under the conditions of those rational relations (those *aitiai*) that logically define it. To ask why God did not create spiritual beings already wholly divinized without any prior history in the ambiguities of sin—or of sin's possibility—is to pose a question no more interesting or solvent than one of those village atheist's dilemmas: can God create a square circle, or a rock he is unable to lift? A finite created spirit must have the structure of, precisely, the finite, the created, and spirit. It must have an actual absolute past in nonbeing and

an absolute future in the divine infinity, and the continuous successive ordering of its existence out of the former and into the latter is what it is to be a spiritual creature. Every spiritual creature *as spirit* is a pure act of rational and free intentionality away from the utter poverty of nonbeing and toward infinite union with God. This "temporal" or "diastematic" structure is no less intrinsic to it than is its dynamic synthesis of essence and existence, or of stability and change.

33. The discovery or invention of the "unconscious" in modern thought—well before Nietzsche and Freud, in Fichte and Schelling and their followers, and even before that perhaps in Böhme—may in fact merely have been the rediscovery under a different aspect of the natural will: of, that is, just this infinite spiritual intentionality that forever exceeds the phenomenal intuitions that it makes possible. For that will is always seeking to be fulfilled *as* intentionality by the only intelligible "species" adequate to it: God in himself. Within this always active, always seeking movement of the rational will there arise—as modalities of ascent into God—images, symbols, dreams, the arts, myths. These are all memories of the spirit's last end, anticipations of the spirit's first beginning. Here too, in this primordial movement of the spirit poetically seeking its end, the gods appear in all their glory and mystery, visions are vouchsafed, prodigies are bred; and all excite a yet deeper longing, a more insatiable striving of the unseen ground and wellspring of the spirit within us toward the infinite and inexhaustible ground and wellspring of the Spirit in and by whom we are created: the fullness of God's own being.

34. If the free assent of the spiritual creature to and in its own creation is, again, nothing other than that final act of joyous confession and praise that is at once both the culmination of the creature's temporal nisus and the eternal origin of the creature's existence, then universalism is not merely entailed, but is in fact a necessary premise for any coherent account of spiritual creation. For, of course, only a "saved" and deified will can, with full rational autonomy, make that confession. No spiritual creature could possibly exist except as "saved," as a god in God.

35. This free confession is, in its eschatological realization, also the corporate free assent to existence on the party of the "Adam" of the first

creation, who from the perspective of time exists only at the end, but who *sub specie aeternitatis* is the eternal creaturely dimension of the divine humanity. And, of course, creation's ultimate confession can be total only by way of a total unity, since a fully moral affirmation of God's goodness—and so a full surrender to God—requires that this rational consent not be inhibited by any "regret" over unredeemed spiritual natures. Finite spirits are not monads, but are constituted in and by their communion in the eschatological fullness of the Adam of the first creation, which is a unity of coinherent love.

36. All these conclusions, it seems clear, follow from Genesis 2:7; there life is imparted to human beings directly by God, breathing his Spirit (*neshamah*) into his creature. Bulgakov is surely right, and on the soundest scriptural ground, when he speaks of the human spirit as that which is uncreated in humanity, and that which proceeds from God as an outpouring from his essence; and Bulgakov is right also in saying that, in creation, God calls his own breath to hypostatic existence—calls his own Spirit to indwell his creatures as their spirits—and thereby gives hypostatic life to the rays of his own glory.[30] As Eckhart says, "Hie ist gotes grunt mîn grunt and mîn grunt gotes grunt."[31] This is the ultimate reason that the first moment of the creature's being is at once a vocation issued by God and yet *also* an act of free self-positing on the part of the creature. Just as the Holy Spirit is not some limited psychological individual consciousness possessed of an isolated self, who is first himself and who then only latterly assents to the Father's self-utterance in the Logos, but is instead hypostatic as God's own eternal assent to and delight in his own essence as manifested in the Son; so also the spirit in us is nothing but a finite participation in that eternal and infinite act of divine affirmation and love. The spiritual creature exists as always, in its origin and its end, wholly surrendered to God. And the chiasmus of the Spirit in us, in our creation and deification, is always the Spirit rejoicing in the love of Father and Son. The inmost reality of the spirit in each of us, that is, is nothing but that act of joyous accord with and ecstatic ascent into God. This is what Maximus identifies as our "natural will," which is nothing but our absolute preoccupation with the supernatural end intrinsic to our very being, more primordial and more ultimate than the transient and finite preoccupations of the psychological ego. In the

eternal act of creation, God's will that the creature be is always already the will of the spirit within the creature to assent to that eternal vocation, because that assent exists within the divine Spirit's eternal response to the Father; every creaturely spirit freely wills its own existence only as a created inflection of God's eternal "I AM" in the mystery of the Trinity. The creaturely spirit's freedom is, in its essence, the freedom of the Holy Spirit within the divine life. The eternal Yes of God to the creature is always already the creature's eternal Yes to its creator, for the latter exists only within the eternal Yes of the Father to his own image in the Son, in the delight of the Spirit; and this is the Son's Yes to the will of the Father; and this is also the Spirit's eternal Yes to the Father's full expression in the Son; and, in the end, these are all one and the same Yes.

NOTES

ONE   Waking the Gods

1. Maximus the Confessor, *Ambigua* VII, PG 91: 1088C–1088D. [For what could be more desirable to the worthy than theosis, according to which God—united to Gods who have come to be—makes everything his own through his own goodness? And hence this condition—born from divine contemplation and then from the elation of happiness—is rightly called delight and affection and joy: delight, on the one hand, inasmuch as it is the end of all natural activities (for this is the definition of delight). . . .]

2. Thomas Aquinas, *Summa contra gentiles* [hereafter *SCG*] III.57.

3. Thomas, *SCG* III.50.

4. Thomas Aquinas, *De veritate* q. 10, a. 11 ad 7.

5. See also Thomas Aquinas, *Scriptum super sententiis magistri Petri Lombardi* [hereafter *Super sent.*] IV, d. 49, q. 2, a. 7; *ST* I, q. 12, a. 1; *Summa Theologiae* [hereafter *ST*] I-II, q. 3, a. 8; *ST* I-II, q. 113, a. 10; *ST* III, q. 9, a. 2 ad 3; *SCG* III.25; *SCG* III.48–54; *Compendium theologiae* [hereafter *Compendium*] I.104; etc.

6. Denis, *De puritate et felicitate animae* a. 56.

7. Aristotle, *De caelo* II.290a.

8. Cajetan, *Commentaria in primam partem* q. 12, a. 1, n. 10. This is a classic example of the confusion of the concept of natural potency with that of an inherent and sufficient intrinsic faculty for the actuation of that potency. See below.

9. Cajetan, *Commentaria in primam partem* q. 12, a. 1, n. 9. Again, the same category error as in n. 8, albeit from the opposite direction.

10. I assume it is not the *sole* possible reading of Thomas at any rate, at least not by the time of the *Summa contra gentiles* and the *Compendium*. That said, I realize that there are places in Thomas's work where a certain interval of arbitrariness between God and his work in creation seems to emerge like a menacing

specter from this or that shadowy corner, such as in his infralapsarian account of Christ's incarnation (*Super sent.* III, d. 1, q. 1, a. 3; *Super primam epistolam ad Timotheum* I.15. 4; *ST* III, q. 1, a. 3), or in his seeming willingness to separate in principle the necessity of God willing his own goodness from the rationale determining the particular goodness he wills in creation (*ST* I, q. 19, a. 3 ad 4; *ST* I, q. 19, a. 4; *ST* I, q. 19, a. 10). Neither of these aspects of his thought, needless to say, is a radical departure from the tradition on his part; but, in his case, both lead to the consequent claim that God created this particular world not as the most fitting or best for revealing his nature, inasmuch as all worlds fall equally and infinitely short of his glory and so any he might create—even if it be much "better" than the world that actually exists—is a matter of pure liberty of choice on his part (*ST* I, q. 25, a. 6 ad 3). All of which is potentially quite distressing. Surely, one has to think, while it is true that there can be no best of all possible worlds in terms of some particular quantity of perfections or some Leibnizian balance between maximal beatitude and the finite conditions necessary to achieve it, it must also be the case that there is nothing truly arbitrary in the way in which God acts and reveals himself, and that therefore he creates this world precisely because it is the world of Christ, the one world whereof the incarnation of the divine Logos is the mystery hidden from the ages, and therefore the one world wherein the consummate revelation of God to his creatures occurs. Even so, none of this in itself makes it logically implausible for Thomas to have believed that any rational creature, no matter what world that creature may inhabit, must be moved by a natural desire for union with God in order to be rational. As I say, though, it is ultimately a matter of indifference to me what Thomas's final view on the matter was, or even whether he had one.

11. Thomas Aquinas, *In Boethii De trinitate* [hereafter *In Boeth. de trin.*] q. 6, a. 4 ad 5; *De veritate* q. 8, a. 3 ad 12; *De veritate* q. 24, a. 10 ad 1; *De malo* q. 5, a. 1; *ST* I, q. 62, a. 4; *ST* I-II, q. 5, a. 5 ad 1–2; *ST* I-II, q. 91, a. 4 ad 3; *ST* I-II, q. 109, a. 4 ad 2; *ST* III, q. 9, a. 2 ad 3; etc.

12. Thomas, for instance, will not allow that the human agent intellect, confined as it is to a kind of knowledge obtainable only through the data of the senses as converted through the phantasm, can actualize the full range of the potential intellect's patient capacity: *Compendium* I.194. But the conditions of the mortal body should not be understood as the natural conditions of the human soul.

13. This applies even to Bernard Lonergan's use of the term "obediential potential" as a sort of amphibologous median between the natural desire for limitless and unconditional knowledge and a supernaturally vouchsafed desire for "quidditative" knowledge of God in himself. It allowed him to explain how a capacity that, to all appearances, seems to be an innate intentionality toward the fullness of God could be understood as continuous with its supernatural fulfillment without collapsing the distinction between the natural and the supernatural

(which, as a kind of Thomist—or, at least, as a faithful child of Mother Church—he felt obliged to affirm). But this is simply a pointless multiplication of conceptual transitions. It is an example of what elsewhere I have called the "pleonastic fallacy": an attempt to span a qualitative disjunction by way of a quantitative accumulation of mediating principles. A creaturely obediential potential that is "natural," even if only in a restricted sense, still cannot constitute a capacity for any end that is not itself also already natural to the creature.

14. It may be worth emphasizing again, given how unfamiliar some of these categories are today even to well-trained Catholic theologians, that the issue here is the abuse of a principle, not the principle itself. I discovered when I first delivered this paper at a conference at Fordham that even many of the Thomists in the room were not entirely sure what the difficulty was. Some of those present, for instance, clearly confused *potentia obœdientialis* with a species of material potency—that is, the patiency of any "material" substrate to an informing cause—and therefore did not see the contradiction in attempting to use it as an explanation for God accomplishing the transformation of a creature into something for which it has no natural aptitude whatsoever while somehow also not annihilating that creature as the creature it is in itself.

15. See David Braine, "The Debate Between Henri de Lubac and His Critics," *Nova et Vetera*, English ed., 6, no. 3 (2008): 543–90. See also Nicholas J. Healy, "Henri de Lubac on Nature and Grace: A Note on Some Recent Contributions to the Debate," *Communio*, English ed., 35, no. 4 (2008): 535–64. Both Braine and Healy, despite their sympathy for de Lubac, feel constrained to defend him against the charge of having taught that human beings have a claim on God's grace by virtue of their nature. This is unfortunate, given that de Lubac would have been right to teach precisely that.

16. See Henri de Lubac, *The Mystery of the Supernatural*, trans. David L. Schindler (New York: Crossroad Publishing, 1998), 76.

17. Here I agree with John Milbank that *Humani generis* drove de Lubac toward increasingly incoherent formulations, and ultimately to compromises induced by the heavy hand of the magisterium rather than by logic. John Milbank, *The Suspended Middle: Henri de Lubac and the Debate Concerning the Supernatural*, 2nd ed. (Grand Rapids, MI: Eerdmans, 2014), 8.

18. Cited by Milbank, *The Suspended Middle*, xi.

19. Even Lonergan, who should have known better, felt compelled to assert that there is "no internal contradiction" in the proposition that "a world-order without grace is possible to God and so concretely possible." Bernard Lonergan, "The Natural Desire to See God," in *Collection*, ed. Frederick E. Gowe (New York: Herder, 1967), 92. And yet, unless he coyly means a world order devoid of rational spirit (and even then he would have been in error), his own understanding of human rational desire makes such a claim ultimately indefensible.

20. Plotinus, *Enneads* I.vi.4.

21. This solution to the issue was suggested to me by a Dominican philosopher in conversation. It is a preposterous proposition in itself, obviously, as he himself ultimately acknowledged, but it was remarkably revealing that he felt moved to venture it. On the whole, one expects Thomists *not* to flirt with nominalism's *deus absconditus*, and certainly not with a quasi-Ockhamist picture of creation as a revelation of a divine sovereignty consisting primarily in wholly arbitrary power. And yet, it seems, the Baroque Thomist synthesis is very hard to sustain in this context except by way of a certain breach between what is revealed in the necessary structure of creation and what belongs to God's own nature.

22. Maximus, *Ambigua* XV, PG 91: 1220AB.

23. Thomas, *ST* I, q. 62, a. 1–9.

24. Thomas, *ST* I, q. 62, a. 1 ad 3.

25. Thomas, *ST* I, q. 62, a. 7 ad 3.

26. See Sergei Bulgakov, *The Bride of the Lamb*, trans. Boris Jakim (Grand Rapids, MI: Eerdmans, 2002), 3–146.

27. Hence the need, incidentally, to reject Lonergan's distinction between the indeterminate natural desire for the whole of knowledge and a determinate supernatural desire for knowledge of God in himself—a distinction, one feels, that he maintained in his thought only somewhat *contre cœur*. The former is not only a passive capacity or even a condition of mere openness, but is of necessity a real and unqualified intentionality toward the whole of being in all its transcendental perfections and all its infinite unity. Such an intentionality is always already a tacit awareness of its "supernatural" end as well as a natural capacity that (at least, when liberated from the unnatural conditions of sin and death) is always already adequate to the end it seeks. As anything's final cause is always already a real rational relation intrinsic to that thing, and necessarily a real capacity thereof, the full supernatural knowledge of God is always already the intrinsic end of the human capacity intentionally to know anything at all.

28. Nicholas of Cusa, *De venatione sapientiae*, XII.32.

29. Nicholas of Cusa, *De visione dei*, XVI. See chapter 2 below.

TWO   The Treasure of Delight

1. Giacomo Leopardi, *Zibaldone*, §§165–83.

2. Leopardi, *Zibaldone*, §165.

3. Leopardi, *Zibaldone*, §183.

4. Nicholas of Cusa, *De visione dei*, XVI.71.

5. Nicholas of Cusa, *De venatione sapientiae*, XII.32.

6. Nicholas, *De visione dei*, XVI.71–74.

7. Nicholas, *De visione dei*, XVI.71.

8. Nicholas, *De visione dei*, XVI.72.

9. Nicholas, *De visione dei*, XVI.73.

10. Nicholas, *De visione dei*, XVI.74.

11. Nicholas, *De visione dei*, VII.26.

12. Nicholas, *De visione dei*, VI.21.

13. Nicholas, *De visione dei*, VII.28.

14. Nicholas, *De visione dei*, XV.66.

15. Nicholas, *De visione dei*, XIII.53–54.

16. Nicholas, *De venatione sapientiae*, XII.32.

17. Nicholas of Cusa, *De coniecturis*, XVI.157; *De quaerendo deum*, II.33.

18. Nicholas, *De quaerendo deum*, II.33.

19. Nicholas, *De quaerendo deum*, II.33–35.

20. Nicholas, *De quaerendo deum*, II.36–37.

21. Marion has developed the concept of the saturated phenomenon in a number of texts over a number of years. See especially *Étant donné: Essai d'une phénoménologie de la donation* (Paris: Presses Universitaires de France, 1997); *De surcroit: Études sur les phénomenes saturés* (Paris: Presses Universitaires de France, 2001); *Prolégomènes á la charité* (Paris: E.L.A. La Différence, 1986); *La Croisée du visible* (Paris: Presses Universitaires de France, 1996); *Le phénomene érotique: Six méditations* (Paris: Grasset, 2003); *Le visible et le révélé* (Paris: Les Éditions du Cerf, 2005); *Certitudes négatives* (Paris: Editions Grasset et Fasquelle, 2009); *Givenness and Revelation: The Gifford Lectures* (Oxford: Oxford University Press, 2016).

22. Nicholas of Cusa, *De non aliud*, XXII.103.

23. Nicholas of Cusa, *De theologicis complementis*, 9.

24. Nicholas, *De visione dei*, VI.21.

25. Nicholas, *De non aliud*, IV.14.

26. Nicholas, *De visione dei*, IV.11.

27. Nicholas of Cusa, *Idiota de mente*, 3.

28. Nicholas, *De theologicis complementis*, 14.

29. Nicholas, *De visione dei*, XII.48.

30. Nicholas, *De visione dei*, XX.89.

31. Nicholas, *De visione dei*, XX.90.

FIVE   *Geist's* Kaleidoscope

1. Philip John Paul Gonzalez, ed., *Exorcising Modernity: Cyril O'Regan and Christian Discourse after Modernity* (Eugene, OR: Cascade Books, 2020).

2. See, for instance, Cyril O'Regan, *The Heterodox Hegel* (New York: SUNY Press, 1994); Cyril O'Regan, *Gnostic Return in Modernity* (New York: SUNY Press, 2001); Cyril O'Regan, *Anatomy of Misremembering: Von Balthasar's Response to Philosophical Modernity*, vol. 1: *Hegel* (New York: Crossroads, 2014); William Desmond, *Hegel's God: A Counterfeit Double?* (Aldershot: Ashgate, 2003).

3. It is an unfortunate fact of academic history that the modern study of ancient gnosticism—and with it the fanciful concept of gnosticism as a kind of precocious speculative precursor of the most daring of modern German philosophical schools—was inaugurated by Johann August Neander's *Genetische Entwicklung der vornehmsten gnostischen Systeme* (1818), Jacques Matter's *Histoire critique du Gnosticisme et de son influence sur les sectes religieuses et philosophiques des six premiers siècles de l'ère chrétienne* (1828), and (most influentially of all) Ferdinand Christian Baur's immense, brilliant, and often wildly misleading *Die christliche Gnosis, oder die Religionsphilosophie in ihrer geschichtlichen Entwicklung* (1835). The last of these volumes exercised so powerful a sway over subsequent scholarship that even its more unfortunate conjectures remained somehow part of the canonical understanding of "gnosticism" well into the last century, and can still be discerned (if only faintly) even in the works of scholars who should have long been disabused of its errors.

4. The habit of superimposing German idealism upon ancient gnostic beliefs is so deeply embedded in the secondary literature that even as fine a historian of antiquity as Giovanni Filoramo feels free to speak vaguely of a gnostic concept of "theogony" germane not only to the "divine" powers, but somehow to God Most High, and to assert that for gnostic thought in general the action by which the eternal God emanates or puts forth the various aeons and hypostases constituting the heavenly πλήρωμα is also a kind of becoming or advance in self-knowledge on God's part: "This process of emanation, of the progressive issue of the divine substance, by means of which God manifests to himself the totality of his infinite potentialities, is a process of enrichment, but also of impoverishment. Indeed, only by the concrete manifestation of the complex articulation of his potential nature can God truly know himself." Giovanni Filoramo, *A History of Gnosticism* (Oxford: Blackwell, 1992), 59. His only citations in support of this extravagant claim, of course, are from secondary sources, none of which in turn grounds the claim in any of the original texts. Moreover, quite without noticing the contradiction, Filoramo then goes on to provide several quotations and epitomes taken from the ancient sources that demonstrate quite the opposite to be the case.

5. *Nag Hammadi Corpus* [hereafter *NHC*] III.71.13–18.

6. *NHC* I.5.51.8–18; I.5.54.2–23.

7. *NHC* VII.5.119.15–16.

8. *NHC* VII.5.121.20–122.8.

9. Irenaeus, *Adversus haereses* [hereafter *AH*] I.i.1.

10. *Berlin Gnostic Codex* [hereafter *BGC*] XXII.19–XXVI.15; *NHC* XI.2.25–4.19.

11. Irenaeus, *AH* I.i.1.

12. *The Wisdom of Jesus the Christ*, *BGC* XCI.4–7.

13. *The Apocryphon of John*, *BGC* XXVI.15.

14. O'Regan, *Gnostic Return*, 45, 138–48.

15. Here, incidentally, is a good example of how even the apparently most obvious "gnostic" echoes in early modern German thought can be misleading. On the issue of the rescue of the fall and rescue of Sophia or the lower Sophia in gnostic literature and its possible reprise in Böhme and in certain forms of German idealist thought, one must never overlook how radically the earlier and the later renderings of the myth differ from one another. In the extant gnostic literature (in which the rescue of Sophia is usually treated as something already accomplished prior to the descent of the savior), the narrative remains a tale of the liberation of a divine captive from an alien realm; in the later German tradition, the figure or shadow of the figure of the "fallen" Sophia becomes at once a kind of exile *and also* a kind of pilgrim, progressing toward her own redemption through the odyssey of history and created nature, and thus returning to the divine plenitude with the bounty of a "spiritual" wisdom that it would otherwise lack.

16. See my treatment of these matters in David Bentley Hart, *Theological Territories: A David Bentley Hart Digest* (Notre Dame, IN: University of Notre Dame Press, 2020), 371–89.

17. Irenaeus, for instance, mentions "gnostics" anointing the dying with oil and perfumed water to aid them in their impending ascent through the spheres of the Archons: *AH* I.xxi.5.

18. This too Irenaeus confirms: *AH* I.ii.1. See also *The Tripartite Tractate*, *NHC* I.5.65–66; *The Gospel of Truth*, *NHC* I.5.18.11–21.25.

19. I might add, moreover, that if the position that Hegelian theologians assume requires—even if only tacitly, vaguely, and as a logical rather than temporal prior premise—the possibility of some kind of initial indeterminacy in the rationality of history and eternity, and a kind of voluntarist indeterminacy at that, then it enjoys no obvious rational superiority over those "systems" that envisage the possibility of some kind of "libertarian" apostasy from the rational good at the level of secondary or created causality, of the sort that could precipitate a "fall" that is nothing more than a fall, contributing nothing absolutely necessary to the achievement of spiritual reason in either the absolute or the contingent. Admittedly, again, this possibility is diminished to the very degree that one can argue for a kind of Aristotelian rationality at work in the dialectical movement from Concept to Spirit.

20. O'Regan, *Gnostic Return*, 9.

21. In English, the best and most insightful portrait of Arius and of the controversy he provoked is the one found in Rowan Williams, *Arius: Heresy and Tradition*, rev. ed. (Grand Rapids, MI: Eerdmans, 2002).

SIX   The Chiasmus

1. Meister Eckhart, *Predigt* XIII, DW I.201.5–8. [Das Auge, in dem ich Gott sehe, das ist dasselbe Auge, darin dem Gott mich sieht. Mein Auge und Gottes Auge, das ist ein Auge und ein Sehen und ein Wissen und ein Lieben./ The eye wherein I see God is the same eye wherein God sees me. My eye and God's eye, this is one eye and one seeing and one knowing and one loving.]

2. William Law, *The Spirit of Prayer*, Pt. 1, chap. 2.

3. Gregory of Nyssa, *Contra Eunomium* III.i, Gregorii Nysseni Opera [hereafter GNO] II: 32.

4. Gregory, *Contra Eunomium* II, GNO I: 340.

5. Augustine, *De trinitate* VI.x.11–12.

6. See Gregory of Nyssa, *Adversus Macedonianos: De Spiritu Sancto*, GNO III, I: 109; *Contra Eunomium* I, GNO I: 217–18.

7. Irenaeus, *Adversus haereses* [hereafter *AH*], V.vi.1.

8. Irenaeus, *AH*, V.vi.1.

9. Gregory of Nyssa, *In Canticum Canticorum*, GNO VI: 150.

10. Gregory, *In Canticum Canticorum*, GNO VI: XV, 440.

11. Gregory, *In Canticum Canticorum*, GNO II, 68.

12. Gregory, *In Canticum Canticorum*, GNO III, 90–91; *De Virginitate* XI, GNO VIII, I: 294–97; *De Beatitudinibus*, GNO VII, II: VI, 148.

13. Gregory of Nyssa, *De Perfectione*, GNO VIII, I: 189.

14. See Gregory, *Adversus Macedonianos*, GNO III, I: 109.

15. Gregory of Nyssa, *In illud: Tunc et Ipse Filius*, GNO II, II: 21–22; *In Canticum Canticorum* XV, 466–68.

16. Gregory of Nyssa, *Tunc et Ipse Filius*, 22; *In Canticum Canticorum* XV, 466–67.

17. Gregory, *Adversus Macedonianos*, 109.

18. See Gregory, *Contra Eunomium* I, 216–18.

19. Gregory, *Adversus Macedonianos*, 99–100.

20. *Epistula* XXIV, GNO VIII, II: 77.

21. Gregory, *In Canticum Canticorum*, 106; *Adversus Macedonianos*, 98–99.

22. Gregory of Nyssa, *Ad Eustathium: De Sancta Trinitate*, GNO III, I: 13.

23. Gregory of Nyssa, *De Perfectione*, 210–12.

24. See Irenaeus, *AH* IV.vi.6.

25. Irenaeus, *AH* IV.xx.7.

26. Sergei Bulgakov, *The Lamb of God*, trans. Boris Jakim (Grand Rapids, MI: Eerdmans, 2008), 92–93, 137.

27. Sergei Bulgakov, *The Bride of the Lamb*, trans. Boris Jakim (Grand Rapids, MI: Eerdmans, 2002), 85–89.

28. Bulgakov, *The Bride of the Lamb*, 184. See also Sergei Bulgakov, *The Burning Bush*, trans. Thomas Allan Smith (Grand Rapids, MI: Eerdmans, 2009), 30.

29. Bulgakov, *The Burning Bush*, 30.

30. Bulgakov, *The Lamb of God*, 91–92.

31. Eckhart, *Predigt* 5b: DW I.90.8. [Hier ist Gottes Grund mein Grund und mein Grund Gottes Grund./ Here God's ground is my ground and my ground God's ground.]

तत् त्वम् असि

INDEX

analogy of being, 69, 71, 72, 81, 105, 112, 115. *See also* transcendentals: Being

apophaticism, 52, 97–98

Aristotelian metaphysics
    act and potency, 2, 3, 4, 8, 9, 10–11
    causality (*aitiai*), xii, 3–4, 18, 99–100, 116, 121
    —efficient, 16, 116
    —final, 3–5, 7, 8, 10, 11, 15, 16, 18, 32, 81, 83, 86, 89, 93, 111, 116, 119, 121, 128n27, 131n19
    —formal, xvii, xviii, 2, 3, 116
    —material, 3, 11, 116, 127n14

Augustine of Hippo (Augustinianism), 5, 22, 29, 31, 55, 56, 60, 81, 82, 103, 108

Blondel, Maurice, 4, 12, 23
Böhme, Jakob, 81, 82, 83, 122, 131n15
Bulgakov, Sergei, 4, 120–22, 123

Christ, Jesus, xiii, xviii, 18–19, 33–34, 47–48, 51, 79–80, 107, 108, 109–12, 113, 120, 125n10. *See also* God: and the Son

Christianity, and other religions, 110–11. *See also* orthodoxy and heresy

cosmology, late antique, 76, 91–92
    and gnosticism, xv, 73–76, 118 (*see also* gnosticism)
    and the New Testament, xv, 77, 78–79, 86–87, 113–14

creatio ex nihilo, 9, 10, 106, 110, 117, 119, 120, 121

deification (divinization), xvi, xvii, xviii, 4, 6, 7, 8–9, 10, 11–12, 16, 19, 20, 27, 31, 32–33, 34, 40, 89, 101, 103, 105, 106, 110, 111–12, 113, 114–15, 118, 120, 122, 123

de Lubac, Henri, 12, 127n15, 127n17

Eckhart, Meister, 97, 123

fall, doctrine of the, xv, xvi, 6, 8, 17, 58, 59, 60, 117–18, 120–21, 131n19
    in gnosticism, 73–74, 76–79, 80, 113, 117–18, 120–21 (*see also* gnosticism)

Fichte, Johann Gottlieb, 121, 122

freedom (possibility and necessity)
    divine, 80–84, 87, 105, 111–12, 115–17, 119, 125n10, 128n21, 131n15
    human, 13–14, 23–24, 25–26, 82, 115, 119
    —and natural and gnomic wills, 29, 98, 115, 116, 117–18, 122, 123

gnosticism, xv–xvi, 63–95, 118, 130n3, 130n4, 131n17

God
  and apophaticism (*see* apophaticism)
  and divine essence (nature), 13, 20, 25, 32, 33–34, 38, 52, 59, 103, 112, 113, 115, 117, 118, 119, 122, 123, 128n21
  and divine infinity, 9, 20, 21–34, 47, 52, 60, 97–124
  and divine judgment, xiv, 42–43, 45–46, 49–50, 113–14 (*see also* hell; universal salvation)
  and divine kenosis, 47–48, 79, 106, 109
  and divine silence, 51–53, 57, 60, 61
  and divine simplicity (*actus purus*), 16, 30, 32, 33, 37, 115–16, 117, 118, 122
  and the Father, 31–32, 45, 47, 48, 72, 73–76, 79, 91–92, 97–124
  in gnosticism, 73–74
  and the Holy Spirit, 31–32, 34, 55, 72, 86, 89, 91, 97–124 (*see also* spirit, created)
  and the Son (Logos), 18–19, 31–32, 45, 46, 47, 51, 72, 75–76, 91–92, 97–124, 125n10 (*see also* Christ, Jesus)
  and Trinity, 31–32, 47–48, 69, 71–72, 83, 90, 91–92, 97–124
  See also transcendentals
grace, xi, xv, xvi, xvii, xviii, 4, 5–6, 8, 9–10, 19, 20, 31, 39, 43, 72, 75, 79, 85, 86, 107, 127n19
Gregory of Nyssa, 20, 23, 103, 107–8, 120

Hegel, Georg Wilhelm Friedrich, 64, 65–72, 73, 75, 79, 80–81, 90, 92, 94, 104, 115, 116–17, 131n19
Heidegger, Martin, 67
hell (damnation), 42–43, 45–46, 83, 91, 117. *See also* God: and divine judgment; universal salvation

judgment
  and aesthetic taste, 44–45, 46 (*see also* transcendentals: Beauty)
  of God. *See* God: and divine judgment
  rational act of, 40–43, 45

Kant, Immanuel, 36–37, 54–55, 56, 57, 100–102

Lonergan, Bernard, 126n13, 127n19, 128n27

Marion, Jean-Luc, 27–29
Maximus the Confessor, 1, 16, 29, 52, 98, 104, 116, 123

nature and supernature, 1–20, 30–31, 33, 86, 98, 110–11, 123, 126n13, 127n19, 128n27. *See also* Thomism: and *natura pura*
Neoplatonism, xvii, 27, 37, 49, 76
Nicholas of Cusa, 20, 21–34, 98, 104

O'Regan, Cyril, xiv–xv, 63–95
orthodoxy and heresy, xv, 64, 66, 72, 73, 74, 76, 78–79, 83–95, 107

phenomenology, 9, 13, 17–18, 21, 25–26, 27–30, 37–38. *See also* Marion, Jean-Luc
prudence, virtue of, 54–55, 56, 58, 59

Schelling, Friedrich Wilhelm Joseph, 81, 82, 122
spirit, created, xv, xvi, xvii, xviii, 1–20, 38, 105, 106, 107, 108–9, 117, 119, 120–22, 123
  rational consciousness (intentionality) of, xiv, 1–20, 21–34, 37–38, 40, 49, 58, 79, 89, 97–98, 99–100, 101, 118, 119, 121, 122, 123, 125n10,

126nn12–13, 127n19, 128n27 (*see also* phenomenology)
and the transcendental subject and empirical (psychological) ego, 14, 27–29, 37, 97, 100, 123 (*see also* Kant, Immanuel)
See also God: and the Holy Spirit

Thomas Aquinas, xii, 5, 6, 7, 17, 55, 111–12, 125n10, 126n12
Thomism, xi–xiii, xv, xvii, 1–20, 30, 55–56, 82, 87, 110–11, 126n13, 127n14, 128n21
and manualist tradition, xi–xii, 4, 12, 110–11
and *natura pura* (pure nature), xv, xvi, 5, 9, 12–13, 19, 31, 110–11
and *potentia oboedientialis* (obediential potency), 10–11, 19, 127n14
and the "two-tier" system, xi, xiii, xiv, xv, 4, 6, 12, 16–17, 110–11
transcendentals, xiv, 13–16, 17, 18, 21–23, 27, 37–38, 40, 48, 49, 51–61, 97–98, 104, 116, 118, 128n27

Beauty, 16, 27, 35–50, 52, 58, 59, 60, 98, 103, 107 (*see also* judgment: and aesthetic taste)
Being, 26, 27, 30, 32, 38, 39, 44, 48, 49, 52, 58, 59, 60, 67, 97–102, 103, 104, 106, 109, 112, 115–17 (*see also* analogy of being)
—iconicity of, 25, 29–30, 33, 50, 51–52, 104
the Good, 13, 14, 15, 16, 23, 27, 37, 38, 45, 58, 59, 60, 74, 98, 119, 125n10
intelligibility (form), 13, 15, 16, 17, 23, 33, 52, 100–102, 103, 104, 109, 122
Truth, 15, 16, 17, 23, 27, 30, 37, 38, 51–61, 98
Unity (the One) 16, 27, 37, 38, 60, 118 (*see also* God: and divine simplicity)

universal salvation, xviii, 46, 122. *See also* God: and divine judgment; hell

voluntarism. *See* freedom

Photo by Nicole Waldron

DAVID BENTLEY HART is a religious studies scholar and a philosopher, writer, and cultural commentator. He is the author and translator of twenty-one books, including the award-winning *Theological Territories: A David Bentley Hart Digest* (University of Notre Dame Press, 2020).